How to Catch
a Crab

How to Catch a Crab

How to Catch a Crab

by

WILLIAM RANDOLPH POPPKE

STEIN AND DAY/*Publishers*/New York

First published by Stein and Day 1977
Copyright © 1976 by William Randolph Poppke
All rights reserved
Printed in the United States of America
Stein and Day/*Publishers*/Scarborough House,
Briarcliff Manor, N.Y. 10510

Library of Congress Cataloging in Publication Data

Poppke, William Randolph.
    How to catch a crab.

    Bibliography: p. 128
    1. Crabbing. 2. Cookery (Crabs) I. Title.
SH400.5.C7P66   639'.54'2   76-53084
ISBN 0-8128-2248-X
ISBN 0-8128-2249-8 pbk.

DEDICATION

This book is dedicated. . .

Firstly, to all edible crabs:
The large, the small, the male, the female, and to each and all that have been, are now, or will exist in the future.

Secondly, to all crabbers:
Past, present and future; Outdoorsmen and nature lovers who have or will have an appreciation of the sport, the challenge, the pleasures, the suspense, the satisfaction, and the accomplishment of catching edible crabs under any and all circumstances and conditions.

Thirdly, to all Gourmets:
Those special people who can perceive the unmatched delight in "picking" and eating the succulent, taste defying, sweet delicate meat that these crabs offer we humble Homo sapiens.

IN SUMMATION:
To the Eternal One who created all nature and all life.

ACKNOWLEDGEMENTS

When a person becomes involved in writing a book, he must, of necessity, contact and request assistance from a great many people in all walks of life, strangers as well as friends. To my pleasant surprise, of the many hundreds of people I contacted, all were completely and genuinely receptive to my requests. They not only gave me whatever help I needed but enthusiastically, freely and willingly offered much much more. Without exception, everyone gave of themselves; a real tribute to all the wonderful people everywhere. I am indeed fortunate and deeply grateful.

Although it is impossible to mention each and every one of these beautiful people by name, they will always be remembered and forever be present within, among and between the pages of **How To Catch A Crab.**

Special thanks, however, must be accorded the following: Charles Breunninger, my grandfather and teacher.

W. A. Van Engel, Chief Marine Scientist, Virginia Institute of Marine Science, Gloucester Point, Virginia, for his vast knowledge and his dedication to the study of crabs and crabbing on the East Coast.

P. T. Hambelton, his mother and his cousin, long time commercial crabbers, Bozman, Maryland, who opened their hearts, their doors, their books, their records, and the Chesapeake Bay to me.

Virginia Todd Corbett, Author, Athens, Georgia; a willing, untiring, competent typist and confidante.

All the students and teachers of the South Orange-Maplewood, New Jersey schools who aided me in a study survey on crabs and crabbing.

Last but not least, Charles Walter Tisch, my friend and crabbing companion. A very careless crabber, always bitten by one or more crabs on **every** crabbing trip; but "Charlie Bleeding Fingers" was the catalyst who constantly supplied a "basket full" of laughs as well as a basket full of crabs.

DEDICATION

This book is dedicated. . .

Firstly, to all edible crabs:
The large, the small, the male, the female, and to each and all that have been, are now, or will exist in the future.

Secondly, to all crabbers:
Past, present and future; Outdoorsmen and nature lovers who have or will have an appreciation of the sport, the challenge, the pleasures, the suspense, the satisfaction, and the accomplishment of catching edible crabs under any and all circumstances and conditions.

Thirdly, to all Gourmets:
Those special people who can perceive the unmatched delight in "picking" and eating the succulent, taste defying, sweet delicate meat that these crabs offer we humble Homo sapiens.

IN SUMMATION:
To the Eternal One who created all nature and all life.

ACKNOWLEDGEMENTS

When a person becomes involved in writing a book, he must, of necessity, contact and request assistance from a great many people in all walks of life, strangers as well as friends. To my pleasant surprise, of the many hundreds of people I contacted, all were completely and genuinely receptive to my requests. They not only gave me whatever help I needed but enthusiastically, freely and willingly offered much much more. Without exception, everyone gave of themselves; a real tribute to all the wonderful people everywhere. I am indeed fortunate and deeply grateful.

Although it is impossible to mention each and every one of these beautiful people by name, they will always be remembered and forever be present within, among and between the pages of **How To Catch A Crab.**

Special thanks, however, must be accorded the following: Charles Breunninger, my grandfather and teacher.

W. A. Van Engel, Chief Marine Scientist, Virginia Institute of Marine Science, Gloucester Point, Virginia, for his vast knowledge and his dedication to the study of crabs and crabbing on the East Coast.

P. T. Hambelton, his mother and his cousin, long time commercial crabbers, Bozman, Maryland, who opened their hearts, their doors, their books, their records, and the Chesapeake Bay to me.

Virginia Todd Corbett, Author, Athens, Georgia; a willing, untiring, competent typist and confidante.

All the students and teachers of the South Orange-Maplewood, New Jersey schools who aided me in a study survey on crabs and crabbing.

Last but not least, Charles Walter Tisch, my friend and crabbing companion. A very careless crabber, always bitten by one or more crabs on **every** crabbing trip; but "Charlie Bleeding Fingers" was the catalyst who constantly supplied a "basket full" of laughs as well as a basket full of crabs.

PREFACE

Fifty years ago, on a brilliantly beautiful, clear and cloudless day in August, my grandfather, a superior sportsman, first introduced me to a crustacean called the blue claw crab. He then commenced to indoctrinate me into the art of crabbing. Little did I realize that this memorable, special event in my life would eventually result in the writing of this book on crabs and the art of crabbing.

A wonderful, continuing adventure began to ensue and unfold from the moment I dropped my baited line into the water. At the time, however, I only knew that I was filled with an electrifying exhiliration I had never before experienced. The very thought of catching a crab engendered strange and fascinating scenes and images in my very young and vivid imagination. The love of this suspenseful, exciting sport was spontaneous and enduring.

Feeling the tug, ever so delicately on the line, then, slowly, slowly, hand over hand inching my adversary closer and closer to the surface of the water was spellbinding. I dared not breathe for fear of somehow exploding within, so I agonizingly contained my impulse to jerk the line straight up in a hurry in order to capture this clawing creature of the deep. While in this state of suspended stress and excitement, I clearly remembered my grandfather's simple but emphatic instructions concerning patience. I, therefore, restrained this almost uncontrollable impulse and continued to slowly maneuver this yet unseen arthropod higher, closer, up, up, up until at last I could see, near the top of the water, this hungry blue claw crab chewing ferociously at my bait. My excitement at this point was intense and only seconds from the breaking point; then, in a flash, this sea animal was scooped into a net and dumped gently into a basket by my experienced teacher, Grandfather.

Words cannot express how very proud I was; but naturally, the conquest overpowered my previously forced restraint and I immediately shouted wild, enthusiastic utterances of joy. The thrill was totally indescribable. Only personal involvement can ever explicate this phenomenal experience.

Since my first encounter with crabs and crabbing as described previously, I have followed the sport through fifty years in and over many and numerous waters — rivers, bays and estuaries from New York south to Florida and from California north to Alaska. Each and every adventure has added greatly to my personal pleasure and knowledge bank. Now, I feel it is time to share these vast accumulated experiences with you, my readers. To my knowledge, no other book has ever been written on this subject and it is my sincere hope that someday, sometime, you too may experience the wealth of pleasures and benefits that crabs and crabbing offer.

I believe learning is instilled at birth and remains a trusted companion throughout one's life. I personally am continuously searching for knowledge, as I truly realize that I still have much to learn. Therefore, to all my readers, I make the following statements:

1. **To the experienced crabber:** It is quite possible that after reading the contents of this book, you will find some areas of disagreement. If that be the case, please write to me and give me your views and criticisms.

2. **To the beginners:** If, after assimilating the contents of **How To Catch A Crab**, you have a question or questions on any of the varied subject materials, kindly do not hesitate to write me for an answer. I will faithfully and diligently try to oblige.

3. **TO ALL READERS:** You are, at any time, cordially invited to correspond with me concerning the contents of this book.

In conclusion:

To each and all — Good crabbing and may your pleasures be many.

Major W.R. Poppke, U.S.M.C. (Ret.)
Maplewood, New Jersey 07040

BY WAY OF INTRODUCTION

Crabbing is a sport that knows no age barrier. Whether six or sixteen, eight or eighty, it is a fun sport for anyone who wishes to learn and try his luck.

It is easy, it is simple, and it is inexpensive. Tie a weight and a piece of bait on one end of a long string and drop them into the water (holding on to the other end, of course). Allow them to go to the bottom and then wait. Know what? You are crabbing! You may or may not catch a crab — but you are crabbing!

To catch a crab, lots of crabs, requires more facts and more knowledge and that is exactly what this book is all about! First, you must know about your adversary, the crab; then, you must employ the proper methods and techniques in his capture; and finally, to complete the rewards and benefits, you must know how to cook and eat nature's epicurean treat.

The wordage used to describe and explain the facts about crabs and crabbing in this book, from beginning to end, has been simplified so that the reader, regardless of age or educational background, can fully and completely understand and comprehend the printed contents. Scientific and technical terms and usages have been omitted and layman's language substituted wherever possible and applicable.

Readers interested in furthering their knowledge in other various scientific studies of this animal are referred to the bibliography as shown on the last page of this book.

Nature's wonders and bountiful wealth are yours to share whenever, wherever and if ever you wish.

All diagrams were drawn by the author who does not profess to be an artist.

TABLE OF CONTENTS

PART I — CRABS

CHAPTER 1

GENERAL BACKGROUND

The crab, a member of the Crustacean class, belongs to a vast assemblage of animals known as arthropods or joint-limbed animals. These animals have been on this planet for millions of years with very little change in original form. They are known to be the most successful of all groups of animals in numbers of their species, in total numbers of individuals, and in their geographical distribution. It is, therefore, quite correct to say, "Crabs are found practically everywhere on earth." It is obvious, after making the above statement, that to mention and describe each and every species of crab by name would be next to impossible. However, the general background information explained herein is applicable to the great majority of crabs. All detailed information and diagrams will be specifically directed to the edible crabs found on the east and west coasts of the United States, for it is these crabs that you will most likely encounter, catch, and observe at the epicure's table.

When a crab egg is hatched, it appears in the form of a tiny grotesque Zoea larvae and is sometimes referred to as surface plankton. This tiny larvae goes through a number of growth and change stages before it even resembles a crab. The whole surface of the body is enclosed in an external skeleton and is therefore designated as an invertebrate animal.

While an external skelton has many advantages, it does have one great disadvantage; i.e., once it has been laid down, it becomes impossible for the animal within to grow in size. It is necessary, therefore, for it (the exoskeleton) to be shed periodically and be replaced by a slightly larger one. This, then, is how the crab must grow and become larger. (See detailed process in Chapter 3 regarding moulting, shedding, and growth.)

The appendages (legs) of the crab are responsible for locomotion, both swimming and walking, as well as for obtaining food. Crabs can swim rapidly sideways, backward and forward. The appendages may also behave as sense organs and provide a sense of balance. These sense organs can detect the presence of various substances in the surrounding water and thereby are attracted to food or can sense danger. Crabs are the scavengers of the sea. They eat a variety of living plants and animals (fish), but their principle food seems to be dead animals. (See Chapter 5). One thing to note with the claws and appendages of a crab is that, as a means of escape or when they detect danger, they can sever (release) their claws or limbs by their own action. However, this is not a lasting inconvenience to them as they can regenerate (grow back) another claw or leg within the next several moults. It is not unusual to catch a crab which is missing a claw or an appendage or where either is in its growing stage and not fully formed.

At one time, Spanish fishermen used to remove the claws of the crabs they caught (claws had high commercial market value) and then throw the live crabs back into the water to regenerate new claws. This method is employed by fishermen catching stone crabs in Florida and is regulated by state laws (see Chapters 7 and 8).

Crabs are quick and can bite or pinch with their claws. Although they seldom do more than draw a little blood, the bite can momentarily be painful. Therefore, it is important to use caution and to know how to handle a crab. (See Part II, Chapter 1).

Crabs do breathe air and when you see tiny bubbles rising, they are exhaling air. Some crabs live on land (land crabs) and return to the water only to spawn (see Chapter 7). The crabs on the East and West Coasts are found in the water, but they can live out of water for some time (Part II, Chapter 1).

The eyes of the crab can be laid back in their sockets in the front of the head for protection. The eyes of the horseshoe crab, for example, are now being studied and scientists have found that each eye contains 500 elongated cones, the most efficient collector of light known. It is quite possible that someday scientists may use this information to develop and manufacture a similarly constructed eye to collect solar energy in the future.

Crabs vary in color. The male blue claw crab (Callinectes sapidus), found on the East Coast, is a greenish-brown with blue claws. The female has orange points. When cooked, crabs turn completely red. Dungeness crabs (Cancer magister) on the West Coast are also greenish brown in color, and when cooked they too turn an orange-red. The red or rock crab (Cancer productus) on the West Coast is red and when cooked turns a darker red.

The normal life expectancy of crabs varies considerably. For example, the blue claw crab lives barely more than three years, while his larger cousin, the Dungeness crab, lives about eight years.

Crabs also vary in size and weight when fully grown. A large blue claw crab might attain the weight of one-half pound. The Dungeness would top three pounds and the spider crab or Alaska king crab may weigh in at twenty-four pounds.

To protect and conserve the crab, every coastal state has promulgated laws and regulations pertaining to the crabs and crabbing in its respective waters. These laws apply not only to the commercial crabbers but to private individuals as well. (See Chapters 8 and 9 for a discussion of laws.)

The crab is an astonishing, amazing and valuable animal. Not only are we using him in laboratories to study his eyes, but, in greater demand, is his blue blood which drug companies extract and use to detect certain poisons for use in medical research. However, most people know the crab as a source of food and this fact has been true since the beginning of time. The commercial crab industry in the United States is ranked high in food resources, volume and value. It is a multi-million dollar business.

Atlantic and Gulf Coasts support large fisheries with an annual production in excess of 77 million pounds of hard-shell crabs and over 6 million pounds of soft-shell crabs, making a total of over 14 million pounds of edible crab meat at a value of over 5 million dollars to the fishermen. The West Coast also has its crab fisheries which supply the industries in Washington State with 18 million pounds of crab meat valued at 4 million dollars, Oregon and California with similar figures, and Alaska, with its king crab fisheries, netting 159 million pounds of crab legs in the peak year of 1966. To my knowledge, there are no published figures as to the number of crabs (or pounds) caught by crabbers (private individuals and sportsmen) for home consumption throughout the United States. It is my candid opinion, however, that the annual figure may well reach in excess of a hundred million pounds.

The crab is fascinating! To know him is to catch him and to catch him is to cook and eat him, as has been done these past millions of years. A strange and suspenseful creature . . . An epicurean delight!

CHAPTER 2

LIFE CYCLE

The life cycle of a crab is not only extremely interesting, but the knowledge acquired by its study can be very helpful in locating and catching this animal in his bottom residence during the crabbing seasons (see Chapter 4, **MIGRATION**).

The diagrams depicted in Figures 1, 2, 3 and 4 demonstrate the generalized life cycle of the blue claw crab found on the East Coast from Maine to Florida, and around the peninsula to Texas. Most edible crabs go through similar cycles; however, the Dungeness and Alaskan king crabs of the West Coast vary enough to warrant separate explanations.

BLUE CLAW CRAB (CALLINECTES SAPIDUS)

Each year, usually between May 15 and October 15, but mostly in June, July and August, a new generation (brood) of blue claw crabs is produced. At this time of the year, the adult female crab is either in or has migrated to the more salty waters of the lower bays, near the ocean, and extrudes from 700,000 to 2,000,000 eggs. These form a large mass known as the "sponge" which is firmly attached to the abdomen of the crab (see Figure 1-A). As the females migrate to saltier waters, the embryo within the egg develops and with the accumulation of the pigment in the eyes and body, the eggs become darker in color. For this reason, "sponges" of crabs in the upper brackish portion of the bay are orange or yellow. Those in more saline water are dark brown when almost ready to hatch. A second "sponge" of eggs is produced in the same summer by many of these females and a few may even spawn a third time before they die. All spawns are a result of the same and single mating of the summer before (see Chapter 4).

The young do not resemble a crab. When hatched, they appear in the form of larvae called Zoea or surface plankton and are about 1/100 of an inch wide (see Figure 1-C). After approximately one month, and four moults later, they have grown to a width of 1/25 of an inch. They, the Zoea Larvae, feed on smaller plankton and are in turn preyed upon by many larger plankton and fish. Many thousands are eaten during the first four stages and many thousands more perish when they become entangled in algae and fungi. Also, if the water salinity is not high enough and if the water temperatures are outside the limits of 68^0 to 85^0 F., an increasing number of larvae fail to moult and therefore die, as they cannot grow.

After the fifth moult, the young crab becomes a megalops (see Figure 1-D) and looks somewhat more crab-like. This stage lasts about a week and then it moults again and finally becomes a "miniature crab." The size at this stage is between 1/8 and 1/10 of an inch wide (see Figure 1-E). It is at this time that this "miniature crab" begins to migrate northward toward the less salty water (brackish) up the bays and toward the rivers. By late fall, this crab has shed its shell a number of times and with each shed has grown a little larger. It is, however, still small and immature.

It then seeks the mud on the bottom, buries itself, and spends the first winter there in hibernation (see Figure 1-F). In the late spring, these immature crabs emerge from the mud and begin to move around, moult and grow. By summer, the now adult crab will have moulted about fifteen times (see Figure 2-A). Most female blue claw crabs attain full growth and mate during their second summer when they are twelve to fourteen months of age (see Figure 2-B). However, spawning does not take place until the third summer, almost a year after mating (see Figure 3-A). The female crab is fertilized by the male during the last moult and only when she is soft (soft-shelled) and underneath the male (see Figure 2-B and Chapter 4). The following spring, after hibernating during the winter, she begins her migration south (see Figure 2-D and -E). This sometimes could be as much as twenty or more miles to the warmer waters nearer the ocean (see Figure 2-D and Figure 3-A). The adult male normally remains behind in the deeper channels of the upper bays and estuaries. He may moult three or more times and mate again with another female the following and fourth summer before he dies.

The first spawning of the female occurs during the third summer (see Figure 3-A). The female crab at this time is approximately two years old and usually dies before the next or fourth summer. When ready to spawn, the female seeks shallow and favorable inshore high-salinity areas, which are generally near the mouth of the bay. After the spawning season, the majority of the females reach the end of their life span. They do not grow anymore and before the next summer most have moved to the deeper waters of the ocean or bays to die. It is noted, however, that a few females do live to spawn once more during the fourth summer, but this fact is not common to the majority.

Figure 4 shows one brood of blue claw crabs through their life cycle as to approximate numbers (which vary tremendously with prevailing conditions) and their locations in saline waters as to male and female. Although no definite figures are available, it is fair to estimate that at most, only seven female crabs out of an entire brood live to spawn and die naturally.

14

DUNGENESS CRAB (CANCER MAGISTER)

The Dungeness crab is found only on the West Coast of the United States, ranging from the Aleutian Islands in Alaska to just south of San Francisco, California. This crab is named for a small coastal fishing village in the State of Washington called Dungeness.

Basically, the life cycle of the Dungeness crab is similar to the previously described life cycle of the blue claw crab with the following differences:

1. The Dungeness is of much larger size, attaining a width of up to ten inches. It does not have the long points or spikes on the exoskeleton that the blue claw crab possesses. It is thicker in body and reaches a weight of over three pounds. The largest blue claw may weigh up to one-half pound.

2. Although both species mate in the months of the summer season, the eggs of the Dungeness are hatched the following January, February and March—three months sooner than the blue claw crab.

3. The sexual maturity in the Dungeness is reached in three years, while the blue claw reaches sexual maturity in twelve to fourteen months.

4. Large female Dungeness crabs carry in excess of 2,500,000 eggs in their sponges, while blue claw females carry 700,000 to a maximum of 2,000,000.

5. After the Dungeness eggs are hatched, they go through seven larval moults (one pre-Zoea, five Aoeo, one Megalops) before resembling a crab. The blue claw eggs go through only five larval stages (see Figure 1-C).

6. At the first appearance as a "miniature" Dungeness crab (after seven moults) the size is one-fourth of an inch wide, while the blue claw is only one-eighth to one-tenth of an inch wide.

7. The life span of a Dungeness crab is approximately eight years while the blue crab lives only two and one-half years with a maximum of three years.

KING CRAB (PARALITHODES CAMTSCHATICA)

King crabs are located in the northern Pacific Ocean and Bering Sea. King crabs are not true crabs such as the Dungeness and blue claw crabs. They are more closely related to hermit crabs. These crabs are caught commercially and not usually by crabbing enthusiasts.

However, as in the case of the Dungeness and blue claw, their life cycle is similar. The following differences are to be noted:

1. The legs of the king crabs are jointed to fold back behind the body instead of being jointed forward as are the legs of the true crabs (Dungeness and blue claw).
2. The legs are spiny in contrast to the Dungeness and blue claw crabs whose legs are smooth.
3. King crabs grow as large as 24 pounds in 15 years and measure about four feet (with legs extended).
4. Female king crabs carry an average of only 240,000 eggs.
5. The larvae are planktonic for 40-60 days, while blue claws remain in this state for five weeks at most.
6. Immature crabs form "pods" by piling on each other (defensive protection method). There can be as many as several thousand in a pod.
7. King crabs reach sexual maturity in four to five years.

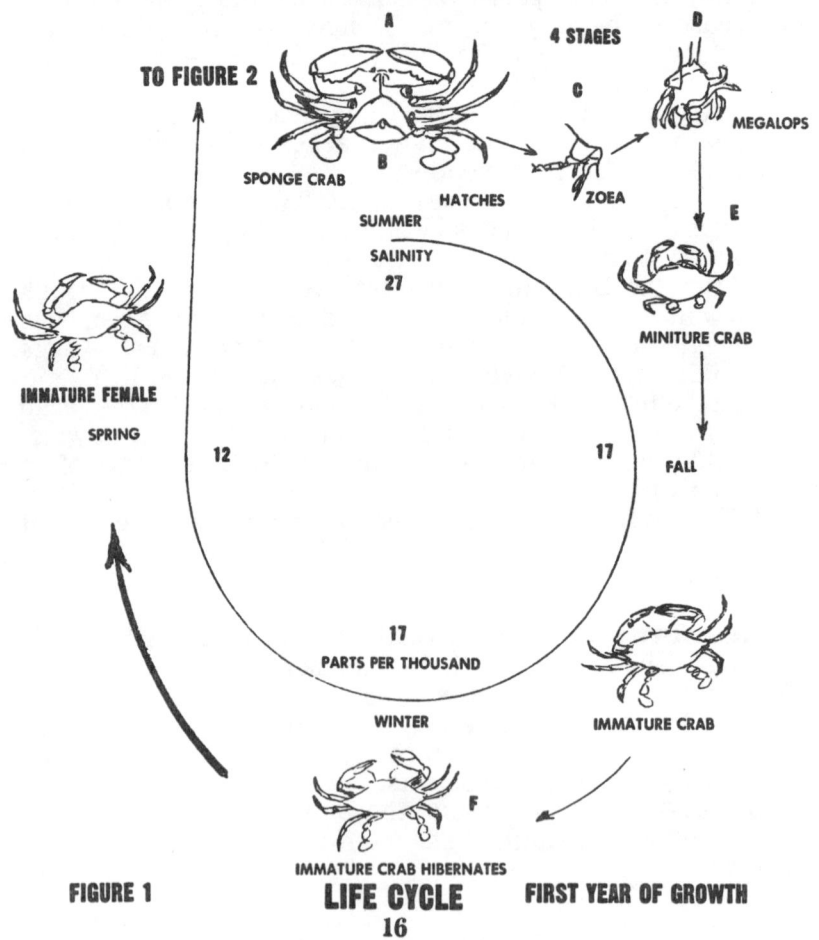

FIGURE 1   **LIFE CYCLE**   FIRST YEAR OF GROWTH

16

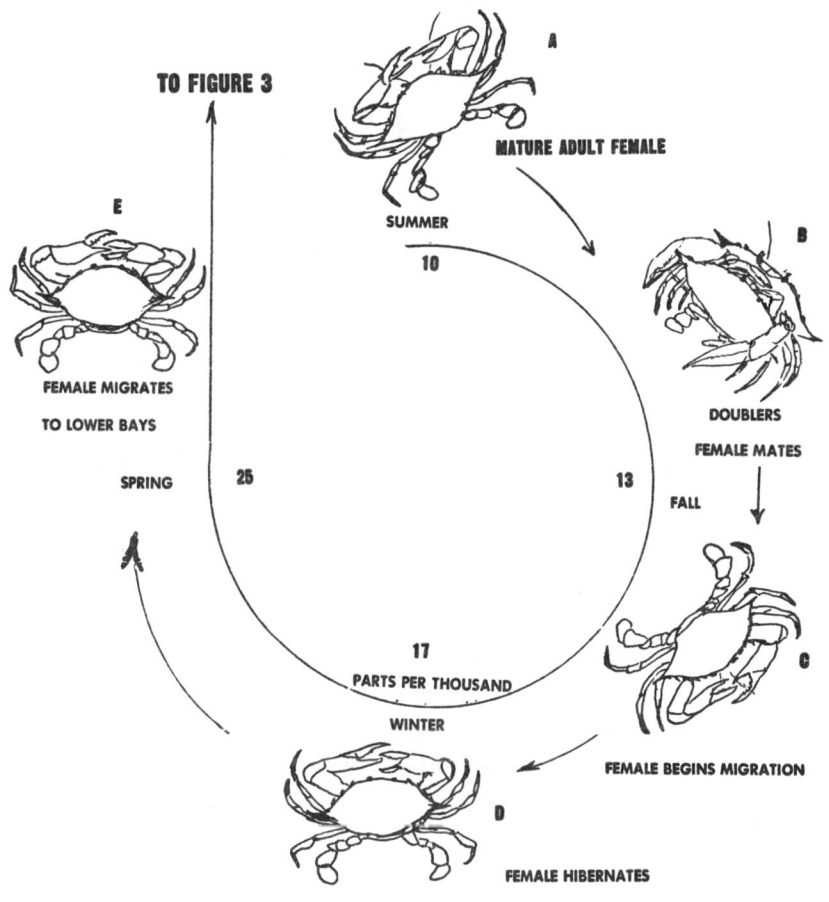

TO FIGURE 3

A
MATURE ADULT FEMALE

E
FEMALE MIGRATES
TO LOWER BAYS

SUMMER

10

B

DOUBLERS
FEMALE MATES

SPRING

25

13

FALL

17
PARTS PER THOUSAND
WINTER

C

FEMALE BEGINS MIGRATION

D

FEMALE HIBERNATES

FIGURE 2   SECOND YEAR OF GROWTH

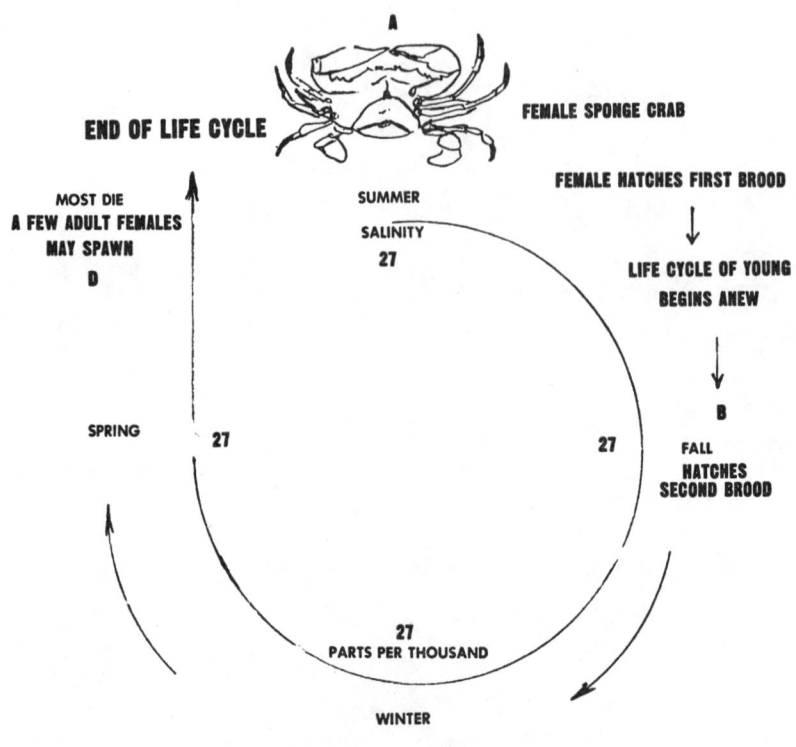

A FEMALE SPONGE CRAB

END OF LIFE CYCLE

FEMALE HATCHES FIRST BROOD

↓

LIFE CYCLE OF YOUNG
BEGINS ANEW

↓

MOST DIE
A FEW ADULT FEMALES
MAY SPAWN
D

SUMMER
SALINITY
27

SPRING   27

27

B
FALL
**HATCHES
SECOND BROOD**

27
PARTS PER THOUSAND

WINTER

A FEW ADULT FEMALES MAY HIBERNATE MOST DIE
C

FIGURE 3   **THIRD YEAR OF GROWTH**

18

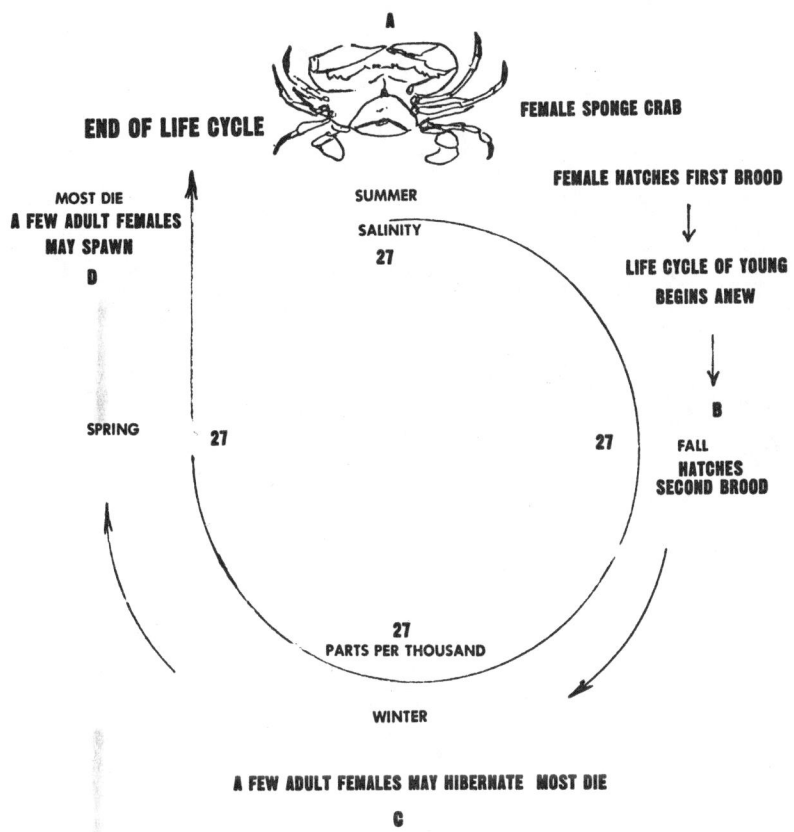

A

FEMALE SPONGE CRAB

END OF LIFE CYCLE

FEMALE HATCHES FIRST BROOD

MOST DIE
A FEW ADULT FEMALES
MAY SPAWN
D

SUMMER

SALINITY

27

LIFE CYCLE OF YOUNG
BEGINS ANEW

B

SPRING   27   27   FALL
HATCHES
SECOND BROOD

27
PARTS PER THOUSAND

WINTER

A FEW ADULT FEMALES MAY HIBERNATE MOST DIE

C

FIGURE 3   THIRD YEAR OF GROWTH

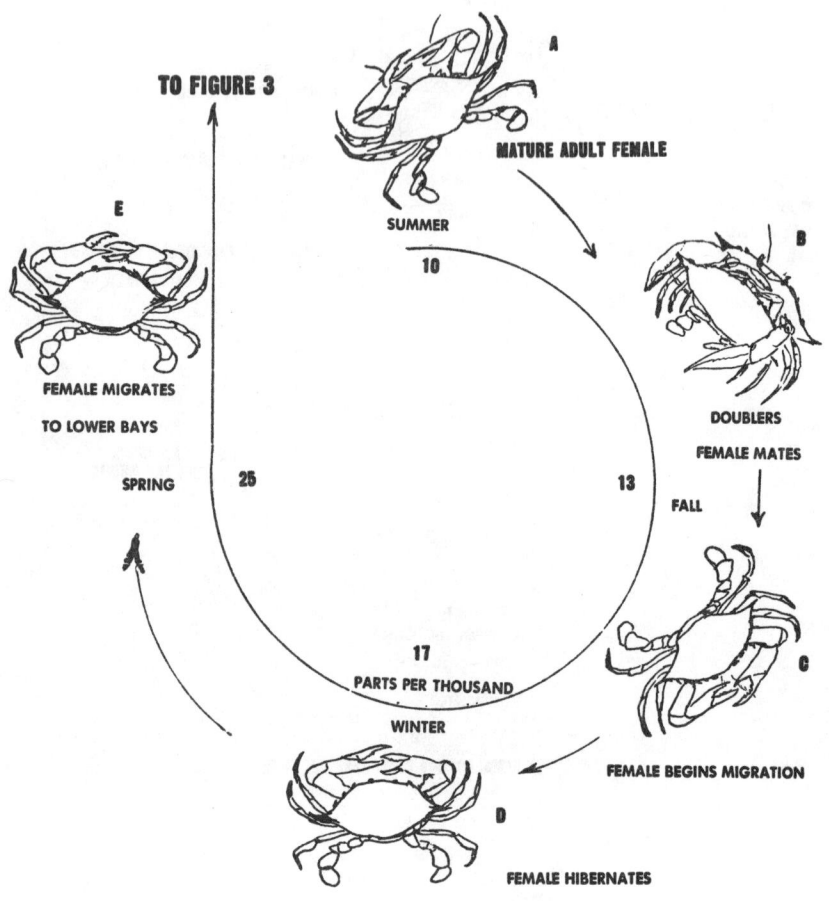

TO FIGURE 3

A

MATURE ADULT FEMALE

E

FEMALE MIGRATES
TO LOWER BAYS

SUMMER

10

B

DOUBLERS

FEMALE MATES

SPRING

25

13

FALL

17

PARTS PER THOUSAND

WINTER

C

FEMALE BEGINS MIGRATION

D

FEMALE HIBERNATES

FIGURE 2

SECOND YEAR OF GROWTH

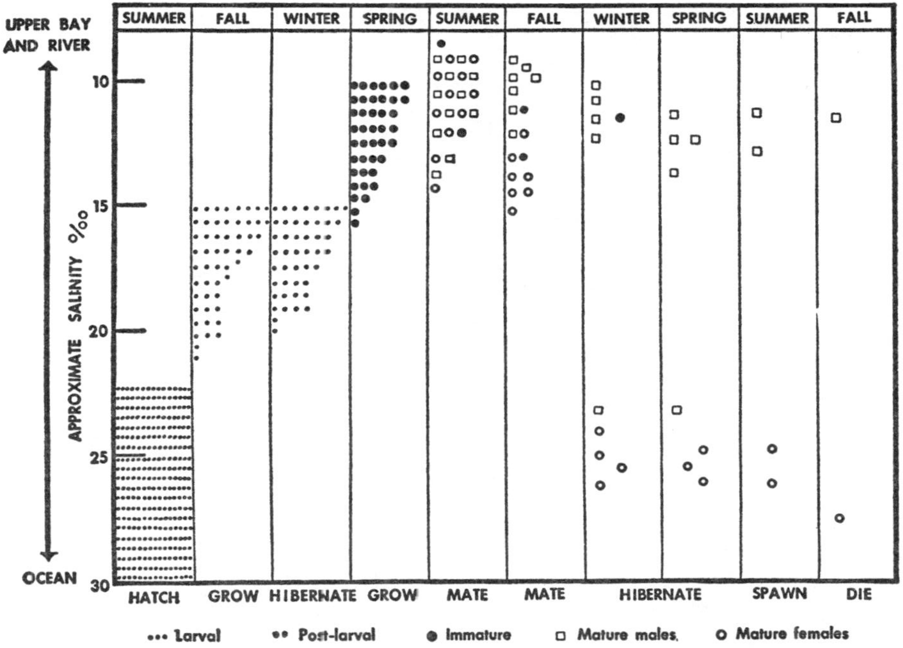

FIGURE 4

HISTORY OF ONE BROOD OF BLUE CRABS

19

CHAPTER 3

MOULTING (SHEDDING) GROWTH, REGENERATION

Moulting is, of course, necessary for growth in an animal which has an external skeleton. The moult serves another useful purpose with crabs in particular. The back (top) of the crab's carapace (hard protective outer covering) offers an especially suitable site for barnacles and other sedentary organisms and many crab shells become encrusted with these parasites and unwelcome organisms. The crab is unable to remove them by its own efforts but when the shell is shed they are all discarded at that time.

As we have seen in Chapter 2, the moment the crab egg is hatched, a process of growing (moulting) takes place. After the larvae and megalops reach the "miniature" crab stage, a female will moult a total of about eighteen to twenty times before attaining sexual maturity. She will then cease to moult, after mating. Males have the same growth pattern, except that they do not cease growth after sexual maturity but continue to moult into the third summer. Since males continue to grow, they may have a total of twenty-one or twenty-two moults, several more than those of the female. Therefore, a full mature (old) male crab will be larger in size than a fully matured female.

The time between moults varies with the size and nutritional state of the individual crab, and water conditions and temperatures. It is also quite probable that light intensity, periodicity, salinity and other external physical factors influence the hormonal balance and, therefore, moulting frequency. Generally speaking (and as a guide), crabs one-fifth of an inch wide moult in three to five days; crabs-one half to one inch wide moult every ten to fifteen days, and crabs three and one-half to four inches wide moult every twenty to thirty days. It is to be noted that the time element between moults increases as the crab becomes larger (Van Engel unpublished data).

Prior to ecdysis (act of moulting), a new shell is formed below the existing exoskeleton of the crab. In order to know when a crab is ready to shed, one must look to the swimming paddles (see Figure 1). Around the outer edges of the last two sections of the swimming paddles are many fine hairs, called setae. A thin, dark brown line representing the outer edge of the hard shell is located at the base of the setae. It is just inside this brown line that the color of the new shell can be observed (see Figure 1-A). The earliest recognizable color state is the "White-Rim" which requires the longest time to shed, usually from one to two weeks. The following stage will be a "Pink-Rim," shedding time to be expected in three to six days. The last stage, or "Red-Sign" peeler crab, will shed in one to three days. "Peeler" is the name given by most fishermen, or watermen, to the "Red-Sign" crab; however, the term "peeler" is sometimes loosely applied to all color stages. Before the crabs shed, they eat ferociously and continuously in order to store food for the shedding process before they can again eat. This process may take up to several days.

In order to free the developing new skeleton from the old, some carbohydrates, proteins, and calcium are reabsorbed from the base of the old shell, and enzymes dissolve away the inner layers of chitin. These carbohydrates, proteins and calcium are stored in the soft tissues of the crab, principally in the hepatopancreas. They may be used for rebuilding and later hardening the new shell. Muscle attachments on the old shell are loosened and shifted to new origins on the future exoskelton. Feeding at this time ceases as much as a day or two before shedding, due mainly to weakened muscles and inability to grind food, and as a preparation for the eventual loss of the stomach lining. When shedding starts, the outer shell cracks along definite lines between the two swimming paddles (see Figure 1-B) and opens up to form a gap between the upper and lower halves of the shell. The cracked shell is called a "buster." When this stage is reached, the crab slowly backs out of the partially-opened old shell (see Figure 2). This process may take hours and is certainly an interesting and wonderful sight to observe. When the crab is completely free of the old shell, it is called a "soft crab" or "soft-shell" crab. It is served in many restaurants as a gourmet's delight. (See Part III).

During the few minutes preceding and immediately following shedding, large amounts of water are taken in by the crab. Expansion to full new size (when all wrinkles in the new skin are smoothed) is completed within about two hours after shedding, and the soft, pliable new shell begins to harden. Over

21

the next nine to twelve hours, the shell begins to take on a papery or leathery texture due to the minerals absorbed directly from the water. The crab is then called a "paper back" or "paper shell." During the next twelve to twenty-four hours the crab's shell becomes stiff and brittle and it is then referred to as a "buckram." The crab does not eat or feed during these stages and another three days will pass before the shell is rigid. Most crabmen refer to the crustacean in this rigid stage as "whitey"; the underside of the shell is very white and the crab is light in weight and meatless. It is at this time that this crab is extremely hungry, eating continually to fill its new shell.

At each normal shedding there is an increase in size of from one-fourth to one-third the initial size (Van Engel unpublished data). For example — if, before shedding, a crab is three inches in width, it then, after shedding, becomes three and three-fourth to four inches in width. If a crab is one inch in width, it becomes one and one-fourth to one and one-third inches in width after shedding.

Environmental conditions do have much to do with the growing process. It has been observed and noted that the increase in body size is due to the absorption of water. Since the amount of water absorbed is related to the salt content of the surrounding water, greater increases in size should occur in water of low salt content (studies have shown that crabs grow larger in tributaries of low salt content and are smaller along the saltier ocean coasts of the eastern shores).

After the female reaches sexual maturity, she moults for the last time and mates with the male while underneath in a "soft-shell" stage. Upon becoming a hard-shell again (usually in three or four days), she begins her migration to the saltier waters of the lower bays and ocean (see Chapter 4).

The regeneration of the claws and appendages of the crab is known as "autogeny." A crab can sever its claws or limbs by its own action when it senses danger or is seeking a method of escape. Also, if any appendage is removed by other causes such as being bitten off by other crabs or fish or removed by humans, the crab can regenerate new claws or limbs. The severance of claws and limbs is not a lasting inconvenience, but studies do show that the loss may affect the growth of the crab itself.

In order for the severed appendage to reach its full size again, it takes several moults. During this period, the crab could be somewhat handicapped in regard to eating and loco-motion and is also more vulnerable to its enemies.

When an appendage is severed, no muscles are affected and the broken ends of the nerves and blood vessels are almost immediately sealed in a blood clot. A miniature limb emerges during the following moult and gets progressively larger with each and every future moult until it again reaches normal size. It is perhaps correct to say that during the life span of a crab many limbs and appendages are lost, and not one crab in the whole world would live a full life without the occurrence of this process.

BLUE CLAW CRAB

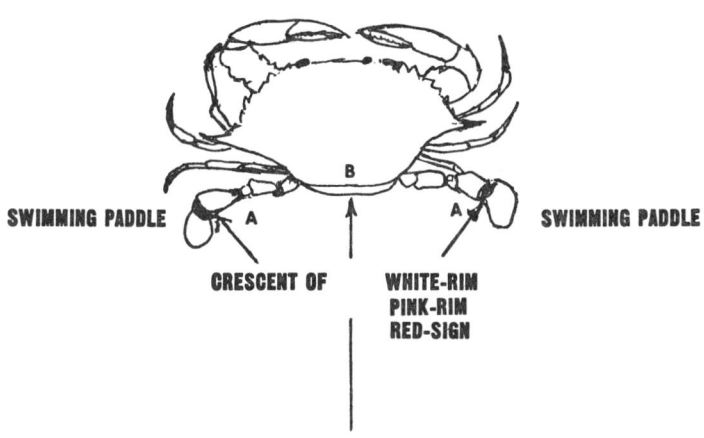

SWIMMING PADDLE

SWIMMING PADDLE

CRESCENT OF

WHITE-RIM
PINK-RIM
RED-SIGN

CRACK APPEARS BETWEEN SWIMMING PADDLES

FIGURE 1   **MOULTING (SHEDDING) SIGNS**

23

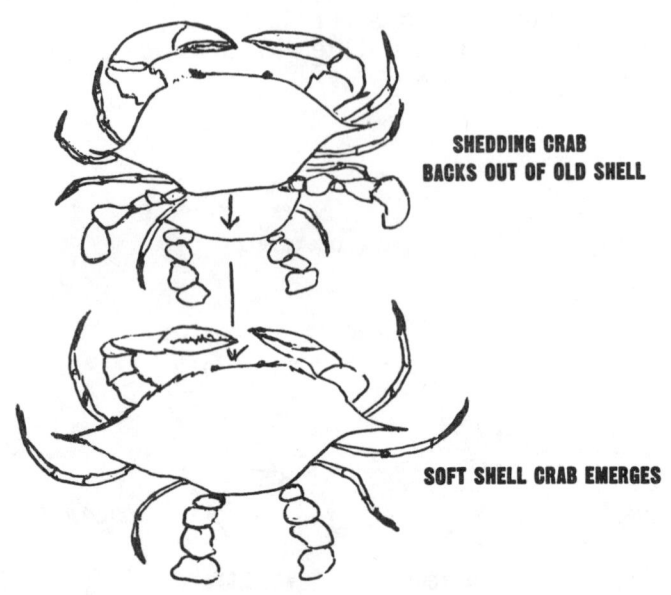

SHEDDING CRAB
BACKS OUT OF OLD SHELL

SOFT SHELL CRAB EMERGES

MOULTING(SHEDDING) PROCESS

FIGURE 2

CHAPTER 4

MATING, MIGRATION, SPAWNING

The sex of a blue claw or Dungeness crab, as well as that of most other species, is easily recognizable by the differences in the shape of the abdomen—or "apron", as it is commonly called (see Figure 1-A, 1-B and 1-C).

The male abdomen is long, slender and T-shaped, and carries two pairs of appendages used in mating: two long intromittent organs and two shorter accessory organs. The abdomen of the immature male is tightly sealed to the ventral (belly) surface of the shell; but on a mating male, the apron hangs or is held in place by a pair of "snap-fastener" type tubercles (see Figure 2-A). In the young immature female, the apron is triangular and sealed to the body (see Figure 2-B). However, in the mature female, this apron is broadly rounded (almost semi-circular) and free of the ventral shell (see Figure 2-C).

The abdomens (aprons) of the young females are grayish-white in color and blue-green in color on the adult females. During the last few days of immaturity and just before the female sheds to become an adult, the dark blue-green of the inner soft adult apron shows through the transparent whiteness of the hard outer immature skeleton.

Young females are sometimes called "Sally crabs." Adult female are referred to as "Sooks". Male crabs are commonly called "Jimmies," Jimmy-Dicks" or Channelers." The latter reach sexual maturity before they are fully grown. During their last three growth stages (moults), they may mate with more than one female.

The mating season normally begins in early May in the warmer waters of the Atlantic Coast from Maryland southward, and continues into October. A female, a few days before her last moult, seeks out a mature male ("Jimmie"). Having found her mate, the smaller female may get on top of the male and hold on to his upper shell with her legs. Soon, however, she goes underneath this same male and he then craddle-carries the female beneath him by hooking his first walking legs and pinching claws between the first walking legs and pinching claws of the female (see Figure 3-A). The female is carried this way for several days until she sheds her shell (last moult). During this shedding process, the male hovers over her. After she sheds her shell, the soft-shell female turns or is turned over on her back and unfolds her apron to expose the two genital pores (see Figure 3-B). Mating may occur day or night and may last from 5 to 12 hours. The male sperm, called spermatophores, are transported to a pair of sacs in the female called seminal receptacles or Spermathecae. The sperm will live in the female receptacles for at least a year, to be used as often as the female lays eggs. After mating, the adult female is again carried "craddle fashion" beneath the male for another two or more days until the female exoskeleton becomes rigid again. During this period while the male is carrying the female, the pair is called a "Doubler" or "Buck and rider."

The female mates only once in her lifetime and only in the soft-shell state as described previously. Therefore, it is undoubtedly important that nature created this process to ensure the male's presence at the critical moment of shedding. It is also essential that the male be present at this time to protect the vulnerable "soft" female from harm and natural enemies until she is once again able to function as a hard-shell crab.

Soon after mating, usually in four or five days, the female leaves the male and begins her migration south to the saltier waters of the lower bays and ocean (see Chapter 2). Mass migration of schools of "sook" (female mated blue claw crabs) can be observed and plotted down the bays in June and again in August. The female Dungeness crabs likewise migrate to the ocean and bury themselves in the sands of the Razor Clam beaches on the Pacific shores in August.

Migration patterns have been studied and charted over the years by various state fisheries and marine science laboratories by the means of tagging adult female crabs. This process can be done by marking the shells of females, as they no longer shed their shells. Also, many studies have been made from the number of females caught by dredging operations of commercial crabbers in the winter months.

Two to nine months may elapse between mating and egg-laying by the female. For example, if mating occurs in early May, the first egg mass may be laid in August of the same year. As a rule, however, most females mature and mate in August and September. The eggs in the ovaries of each female develop almost to completion within two months after mating, and most of the time egg-laying is delayed until the following May or June. Appropriate names for egg-bearing females are: (1) Sponge crab; (2) Cushion crab; (3) Lemon or Orange crab (because of the color of the sponge); (4) Berry or Berried crab; (5) Ballie; (6) Pink; and (7) Busted Sook. Unmated females may produce sponges of unfertilized eggs but this is usually infrequent and quite rare, as there always seems to be an abundance of males, each capable of mating with several different females.

Some females spawn twice or more. The females that mate in August and September usually produce their first hatch the following May or June, and a second hatch in August. The females in these instances use only a portion of the male sperm which has been stored in their receptacles at each spawning. Egg-laying is rapid and may be completed in two hours (reference: **Commercial Fisheries Review,** Vol. II, No. 6, W.A. Van Engel).*

After a female hatches her eggs, the life cycle of the young larvae begins anew (see Chapter 2).

*Presently the Senior Marine Scientist of Virginia Institute of Marine Science, Gloucester Point, Virginia.

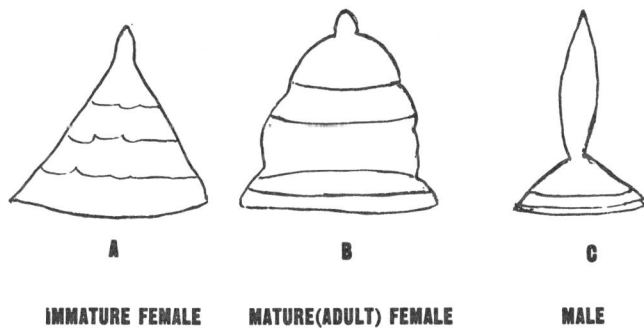

A	B	C
IMMATURE FEMALE	MATURE(ADULT) FEMALE	MALE

FIGURE 1   **ABDOMEN (APRON) OF THE CRAB**

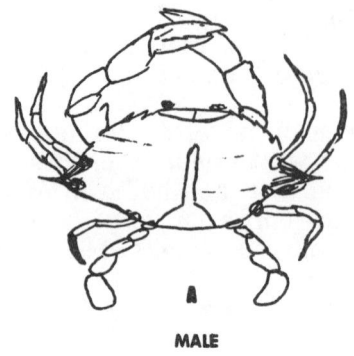

MALE

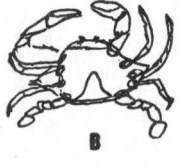

IMMATURE FEMALE

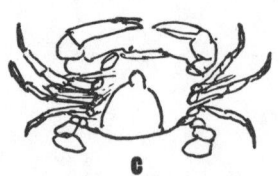

MATURE (ADULT) FEMALE

FIGURE 2   **APRONS**

28

A

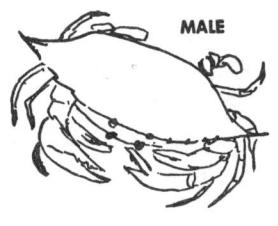

MALE

DOUBLER

BEFORE MATING MALE CRADLE CARRIES ADULT FEMALE

MATURE FEMALE
UNDERNEATH

B

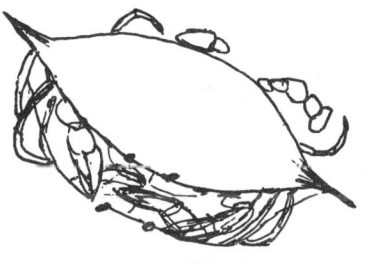

MATING

MALE TURNS FEMALE OVER AFTER MOULTING

FEMALE UPSIDE DOWN

FIGURE 3   **MATING**

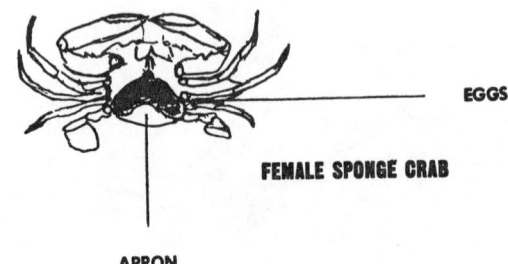

A

EGGS

FEMALE SPONGE CRAB

APRON

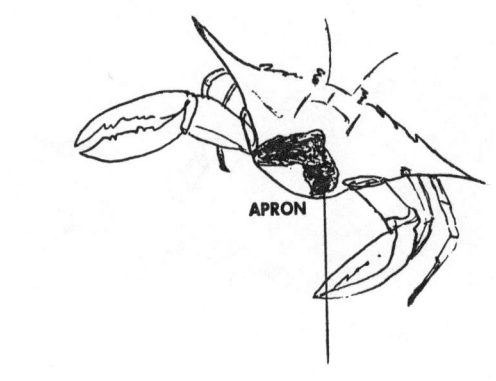

B

APRON

EGG MASS

FIGURE 4

CHAPTER 5

EATING HABITS AND DIET

The crab can be classified as a continuously hungry scavenger. After each moult, the crab is naturally a more ferocious eater than usual; but at all times, except during moulting, he is constantly searching for food to satisfy his enormous appetite. Crabs are always on the move, roaming the bottom, the top, the marshes, the deep and the more shallow areas in a relentless quest for food.

The diet of most crabs is quite variable and consists mainly, but not exclusively, of a variety of living plants and vegetation, plankton, live and dead fish, and other marine forms. Most crabs of all species are highly cannibalistic, the blue claw crab and Dungeness included.

Certain land crabs eat the live young of birds that nest on the ground, terns especially, as well as other live animals. Crabs eat roots, shoots and leaves of common seaweed, eel grass, ditch grass, sea lettuce, salt marsh grass and many other marine plants. The crab will dine on clams and oysters when other food is less available, but the crab is not considered a serious pest or menace in this area of food consumption.

From laboratory studies over the years, it is a proven fact that the Dungeness crab is not attracted to nor will he eat spoiled or putrefied foods. Examinations of the stomach contents of the Dungeness crab have shown evidence of hard-shell and razor clams, fish, crabs, starfish, worms, squid, snails and eggs from fish and crabs.

In addition to plant life, crabs eat mostly dead fish and meat, and are and can be attracted to almost any type of bait. As a point of information, the following partial list of food has been used as bait to catch crabs:

1. Chicken: backs, necks, wings, and entrails.
2. Liver: beef, pork, lamb, cow.
3. Bones: all animals (with some meat attached to bone).
4. Kidneys: of all animals.
5. Hearts: of all animals
6. Slaughterhouse trimmings (raw uncooked meat): aged beef, cow, bull, all parts.
7. Fish: any and every kind, both fresh and salt water species, alive or dead, whole or parts (head, tail, main skeleton with some flesh still on parts), squid and eels.

It is the opinion of the author that no one particular bait enumerated in the list is superior to another; rather, it is believed that the crabs are attracted to the food by their natural sense organs, and eat the bait because of hunger. At times it may be observed that a crab may prefer and be attracted to one of the baits more quickly than to another, but there is no concrete evidence or proof that any one bait is the best to use in attracting and catching crabs. It will suffice to say that all have been used with good results and success.

Normally tough "trash fish" (such as sea robins, oyster crackers, blow fish) eels and slaughterhouse trimmings are preferred when using a trotline, as they hold up better and remain intact for a longer period of time than do soft-bodied fish.

Crabbers using crab pots, baskets, or traps generally prefer to use an oily fish for bait, namely moss bunker, menhaden, mackerel or eel.

With a drop line (bait and weight) anything goes, depending upon your own preference and the availability of the bait. Try them all and make your own deductions and conclusions.

CHAPTER 6

FLUCTUATIONS IN ABUNDANCE
POPULATIONS, EFFECTS

The "catch of crabs" in most areas of the United States has varied tremendously from year to year. For example, in the Chesapeake Bay there have been increases of as much as 31% and decreases of as much as 47% from one year to the next succeeding year.

Although many and various studies have been made in the past, experts cannot actually account for nor pinpoint the wide variations in fluctuations of crab populations. No study thus far has totally proved the causes of these fluctuations and there is no positive evidence that commercial fishing (with crab pots, trotlines or winter dredging) or private sport crabbing, even with the catching and taking of egg-bearing females, has resulted in the lowering of the supply of crabs the following year. Conversely, this does not prove that these practices are not harmful. They could be. It remains mandatory, therefore, that further comprehensive research be conducted by biological and hydrographic scientists and experts.

The important question at present seems to be: "Can crab fishery standards be maintained through conservation methods at any particular level or abundance or is the yearly crab yield solely and wholly determined by natural factors and forces (water salinity, water temperature, food supply, predators, disease, etc.) ?"

The following experimental and informational data, derived from past studies and research, will help to explain some, but not all, of the reasons for and the effects of the abundance and fluctuations of the crab populations:

1. Probably the most important factor affecting numbers of crabs is the salinity of the water (see Chapter 2, Figures 1, 2, 3 and 4). It has been found that the optimum (most favorable conditions for growth and reproduction of an organism) range of salinity for hatching eggs is between twenty-five and thirty parts per thousand. A high mortality rate occurs below twenty-three and above thirty parts per thousand.

2. It is extremely important that optimum salinity for growth of the first three larval stages is twenty-one to twenty-eight parts per thousand. Below eighteen and above twenty-nine reflects a decrease in larval activity.

3. Although spawning occurs on the bottom (where the salinity factor may be within optimum range), the larvae

soon float to the upper layers of surface water and remain there for several weeks. If these upper layers are not in the proper salinity ranges (because of fresh water discharges from the rivers caused by excessive rain in May, June or July), then the mortality rate of the young is tremendously high and hundreds of thousands of them perish at this stage.

4. Excessively cold weather or extremely hot weather (water temperatures in the high eighties) in the spring, summer, fall or winter (during hibernation) can cause heavy mortality in the immature and adult crab population.

5. Lack of adequate food supply (both plant and animal) in the local areas could also have a significant effect on the abundance of crabs and, because the crab is known to be cannibalistic, this too adds to (self-) reduction.

6. Stocks of crabs in one location do not usually mingle with crab stocks of other locations. Normally, they are indigenous to their local surroundings unless dire circumstances necessitate movement elsewhere.

7. An over-abundance in any one year of predators (natural enemies of the crab, such as halibut, fluke, dogfish, blowfish, hake, ling-cod, oyster crackers, great-marbled sculpin, wolf eel, octopus and others) will take a heavy toll of that year's crab population, and affect the next year's abundance.

8. Pollution of the waters and land areas surrounding the waters is naturally a constant threat to all crustaceans.

9. Crabbing intensity and economic conditions may play a part in the scarcity of crabs from year to year.

10. Natural phenomena, such as the earthquake and aftershock tidal-wave which occurred in Seward, Alaska, could wipe out entire areas of crab populations, as was the sad result in Seward; not a Dungeness crab can be found in Resurrection Bay.

11. It is also quite possible that a disease commonly known as "gray crab disease," but actually termed "paramoeba" or "amoebiasis," of which very little is known, may affect high mortality in some locations.

What are the answers? It is the sincere desire of the author that, through continual study and research, all the answers may soon be found. With knowledge, proven facts, and scientific data, this marvelous food-giving crustacean then can be fully protected and can endure to be bountiful for millions of years to come.

CHAPTER 7

KINDS OF CRABS

Crabs are technically classified in the phylum (any primary division of the animal or vegetable kingdom) Arthropoda, class Crustacea, subclass Malacostraca, order Decapoda, suborder Reptantia. The suborder Reptantia is divided into the Macrura (crayfish and lobsters), the Anomura (hermit crabs), and the Brachyura (true crabs); these groups (suborders of Decapoda) are most commonly called sections. A definite classification of the section, Brachyura, has not yet been achieved. Many authorities find it most satisfactory to divide the true crabs (Brachyura) into four groups: (1) Gymnopleura; (2) Dromiacea; (3) Oxystomata, and (4) Brachynatha.

GYMNOPLEURA:

This group contains about thirty species of primitive crabs characterized by a long body and subchelatate chelipeds (the end segment of the leg that bends back against the next segment to form a claw), and by having the remaining pairs of walking legs flattened and expanded to aid in burrowing. The oviducts of the female open on the coxae (top segment) of the fourth pair of walking legs.

DROMIACEA:

This is a group of primitive crabs comprised of approximately two-hundred species that carry a fifth and last pair of walking legs up on the back. The fifth and often the fourth pair of walking legs are short and end in little pincers. They are used for holding an object which presumably serves as a disguise or concealment, over the back of the crab. The object is most often a sponge, which continues to live and grow as it is carried about.

The mouth frame is square. The Dromiacea are slow, heavy animals protecting themselves through concealment rather than active avoidance and defense.

OXYSTOMATA:

In this group of about five hundred species, the mouth frame is triangular and projects forward, joining with the inner lobes of the first maxillipeds to form a pair of closed tubes through which the water from the gill chambers is expelled. The last pair of legs may be normal or may be modified for holding a sponge or an empty shell over the back. Most of the Oxystomata are burrowing crabs, burying themselves in the sand or mud until only their eyestalks show above the surface. The modified mouth is an adaptation for breathing while buried. Some of the Oxystomata strongly resemble spider crabs (Oxyrhyncha).

BRACHYNATHA:

More than 3,700 species, or four-fifths of all the living crabs, belong to this group. The Brachynatha are characterized by a square mouth frame and the absence of the first pair of pleopods (swimmerets), and by the location of the openings of the oviducts on the bottom of the body (sternum). The last pair of walking legs of the crabs in this group are rarely reduced in size or carried upon the back.

This group may be divided into the Oxyrhyncha and the Brachyrhyncha, sometimes called superfamilies, which can be distinguished by body shape. In the Oxyrhyncha, the carapace (shell) usually narrows in front, forming a simple or forked rostrum so that the body is triangular in outline. The Brachyrhyncha have round, transversely oval, or square bodies.

OXYRHYNCHA:

The Oxyrhyncha include the spider crab and related forms. They have very long, thin legs and relatively small bodies. They are good to eat and are located on the European continent. The largest Oxyrhyncha are found in Japan. Outstretched claw span of a full-grown specimen can exceed ten feet (each claw could be almost six feet in length). They are sluggish crabs that live among seaweed or plant-like animals, and depend upon concealment for protection. Their bodies are colored and sculptured to resemble their background, and the carapace is often covered with spines and tubercles. In addition, many spider crabs conceal themselves by covering their bodies with pieces of seaweed, sponge, or other marine growths, which they attach to hairlike hooks on the body and legs. Sticky secretions from glands on the first maxillipeds help to keep these fragments attached also.

BRACHYRHYNCHA:

These are mostly active, strong-shelled crabs that usually defend themselves vigorously. The majority of crab species and the most varied in form are found in this group, namely the blue claw, Dungeness, stone crab, red or rock crabs (swimming crabs), pea crab and land crabs. All of these crabs are edible and several have been discussed at length in previous chapters. However, for information, pea crabs (family Pinnotheridae) are feeble crustaceans with soft bodies and tiny eyes and antennae. Most of them live in the mantle cavities of mussels, clams, or oysters, feeding either by filtration or by ingesting the mucous food strings of their hosts.

The land crabs, robber or cocoanut crabs (family Gecarcinidae) live in tropical regions throughout the world, sometimes honeycombing the ground with their burrows. They are not completely independent of the sea, however, as they must return when the eggs hatch, to release the zoea larvae into the sea.

Lancerpaurus, similar to the land crab (like the ones above) is pinkish or reddish brown like the red or rock crab and has black-tipped claws. It is found offshore in rocks and is caught, like lobsters, in pots. This is a large crab, weighing up to twelve pounds. The liver is firm and bright red and is considered a real gourmet's treat. It is the general consensus of opinion that the male is more flavorful than the female. The carapace (body or shell) is nearly one foot across. Many of these crabs are found around the British Isles.

The stone crab, a true crab, (Menippemercenaria) is very thickshelled and is found along the southern coasts of the United States. The stone crab lives in burrows just below the low tide line from North Carolina to Mexico and along the coast of Cuba. It attains a size of five inches across the back. It once was found in abundance but now is threatened by extinction. Much of the choicest meat is found in the lance claw. Fishermen break this claw off and return the crab to the waters to grow a new claw. (In other parts of the world, Anomura crabs, related to the hermit crab, are commonly referred to as stone crabs but are not in the same section and are not true crabs.

The red or rock crab was partially discussed in previous chapters. It is a hard-shell, true crab of the genus Cancer and is found on the rocky shores and in offshore waters along both coasts (mostly on the West Coast) of the United States. The common rock crab (Cancer irroratus) of the Atlantic Coast ranges from Laborador to South Carolina; the Jonah crab (Cancer borealis) is found from Nova Scotia to Florida. Both of these are edible but are not as tasty as the blue claw or stone crab. On the West Coast from Oregon to the Gulf of California, the red or rock crab (Cancer antennarcius) is found in varied abundance. This crab is related to the Dungeness (Cancer magister), but is not as large and not as flavorful.

Although the hermit crab is not a true crab, but rather a member of the Anomura classification, and is not edible, it would be remiss if this crazy, funny little creature were not mentioned in this chapter. Most of us have observed his antics and must admit he is certainly a busy little fellow. As a shallow offshore water-dweller or as a land hermit, he is constantly looking for a new shell to house in as he grows. He can be seen on the beach busily moving from one empty shell to another in search of his next selected residence. It is not uncommon, however, that the hermit crab sometimes remains too long in the last abode and cannot extricate himself. This situation does not affect his or her mating capabilities, but it certainly puts a curb on future growth.

References: Thomas E. Bowman, Smithsonian Institution and **Colliers Encyclopedia.**

CHAPTER 8
EDIBLE CRABS - EAST COAST
STATE LAWS AND REGULATIONS

In order to protect and conserve fish and wildlife, each and every individual state has promulgated and enacted state statutes (laws and regulations) relating to the fish and wildlife located within the confines of its own state borders and coastal waters. These laws generally govern and pertain to the licensing of residents, non-residents, individual sportsmen and commercial fishermen alike. They define the methods, means and seasons of catching and taking crabs, limits of catches, sizes, prohibitions, fines and penalties. Regardless of where you fish or crab, it is certainly advisable to be fully cognizant of the applicable local state laws and regulations.

Because all state laws are not uniform and vary considerably in scope, degree and detail, the following information is presented as an aid to the crabber (individual sportsmen, not the commercial fishermen). It outlines briefly various state laws relative to the catching and taking of edible crabs on the East Coast, mainly, the blue claw crab and the stone crab.

PRESENT LAWS IN FORCE
(Alphabetical by state)

Alabama: **Blue Crab**

No license requirements or set seasons for crabbing are specified. Size shall not measure less than four inches in width as measured from widest points of upper shell. Possession of crabs of less size is prohibited. There is no limit as to the number of crabs taken.

Connecticut: **Blue Crab**

No license is required. Open season is from May 1 to November 30. Minimum legal-size hard-shell is five inches from tip to tip of spikes; soft-shell, three and one-half inches from tip to tip of spikes. Egg-bearing females must be immediately returned to the water. Crabs may be taken only by scoop net, trotline, hand line, or other device approved by the State Commissioner. A license is required to take blue crabs for commercial purposes.

Delaware: **Blue Crab**

No license is required. Minimum size catch is four inches (shell tip to shell tip). Non-residents shall not use more than four hand lines nor possess more than two hundred crabs at any time. It is illegal to catch or possess female crabs bearing eggs. The use of more than two crab pots by any individual is prohibited.

Florida: **Blue Crab**

No license is required. Crabbing is permissable during any season of the year. There is no prohibition on taking egg-bearing females. No individual can crab with more than five traps.

Stone Crab Regulations:

(1) Season - Size - Sex

(A) It is unlawful for any person, firm or corporation to catch or have in their possession, regardless of where taken, for their own use or to sell or offer for sale, any stone crab whatsoever of any size between May 15 and October 15 of each year, except as provided by Section 370.141, Florida Statutes, for storage and distribution of inventory stocks.

(B) It is unlawful to possess, sell or offer for sale any stone crab at anytime which has a forearm (propodus) of less than two and three-fourths inches in length, measured by a straight line from the elbow to the tip of the lower immovable finger. The forearm shall be deemed to be the largest section of the claw assembly having both a movable and immovable finger, and located farthest from the body of the crab.

(C) It is unlawful to transport by boat, land vehicle, airplane or other conveyance any intact stone crab or stone crab body whether dead or alive. Only the claws of the stone crab shall be removed, and the live animal shall be returned to the water. Whole stone crabs, dead or alive, may be possessed solely for educational, exhibitional or scientific purposes, when a permit for such possession has been issued by the Division of Marine Resources of the Department.

(2) Gear, Traps, Buoys, Permit Numbers, Suspension or Revocation of Permits

(A) No person, firm or corporation shall transport on the water, fish with or cause to be fished with, set or placed, in taking stone crabs, any trap with throat or entrance to trap exceeding four inches in width and six and one-half inches in length.

(B) It shall be unlawful to transport on the water, fish with, set, place or cause to be fished with, set or placed, any trap during the closed stone crab season; provided, traps may be placed in the water and baited ten days prior to the opening of the stone crab season and shall be removed within five days after the close of the stone crab season. However, nothing herein shall authorize the landing or sale of any stone crab or stone crab claw during the closed season. Any traps in the water more than ten days prior to the opening of the stone crab season or more than five days after the close of the season shall be conclusively presumed to be used in the attempted taking of stone crabs out of season and shall be seized and destroyed by the duly appointed officers of the Division of Marine Resources. This provision shall be in addition to any penalty imposed by law.

(C) It is unlawful to use grains, spears, grabs, hooks, or similar devices in the taking of stone crabs.

(D) A buoy shall be attached to each trap and must be of sufficient strength and buoyancy to remain afloat continuously. It must be of such color, hue, and brilliancy as to be easily distinguished, seen and located. The color and permit number shall also be permanently and conspicuously displayed on the boat used for setting and collecting said traps and buoys in a manner prescribed by the Division of Marine Resources so as to be readily identifiable from the air and the water.

(E) Each trap used must have a number permanently attached to the buoy and trap. No numbers shall be permitted other than the current permit holder's number except numbers designating Federal permits. This permit number may be issued by the Division of Marine Resources of the Department of Natural Resources upon receipt of the application by the owner of the traps. The design of the application and permit shall be determined by the Division The trap permit number shall be affixed in legible figures at least three inches high on each buoy used. The stone crab permit must be on board the boat with the operator, subject to inspection, at all times. Only one permit shall be issued to each boat.

(F) It is unlawful for any person to molest any traps, lines or buoys as defined herein, belonging to another without permission of the permit holder.

(G) Any traps or devices other than the one described in this sub-section used in the taking or attempted taking of stone crabs shall be seized and destroyed by the duly appointed officers of the Division of Marine Resources of the Department of Natural Resources.

(H) Upon the arrest and conviction for violation of any of the stone crab regulations or laws, the permit holder must show just cause why his permit should not be suspended or revoked.

(I) Any law, general or special, in conflict with provisions of this section is hereby expressly repealed to the extent of such conflict.

(3) **Penalty:**

Any person violating this section shall be guilty of a misdemeanor of the second degree upon the first conviction. He shall be guilty of a misdemeanor of the first degree upon the second or subsequent conviction, punishable as provided in Section 775.082 or Section 775.083. In addition to the penalty imposed for first or second-degree misdemeanors, any gear, equipment, boats, vehicles or items used in the violation shall be subject to confiscation.

Georgia: **Blue Crab**

There is no license required and there is no set season. It shall be unlawful for any person, firm or corporation to take from any waters of the state, or to buy or sell, or to be in possession of any spawning female crab or crabs. This provision shall **only** apply during the months of May and June in every county having a population of not more than 151,480 according to the 1950 United States Census, or any future United States Census. No person shall take, catch, possess or offer for sale any crabs of less than five inches from spike to spike across the back. There is no catch limit.

Louisiana: **Blue Crab**

There are no license requirements or set seasons for crabbing. Minimum legal size for the hard-shell crab is five inches in width, and for the soft-shell crab it is four and one-half inches in width. Egg-bearing females must be returned to the water alive. It is illegal to trawl for crabs but any other method is legal. There is no limit as to the number of catch.

Stone Crab

No license is needed and there are no specific requirements.

Maine: **Blue Crab**

A crabbing license is required. This, however, does not apply to the taking or catching of crabs with bare hands, or with hook and line that may be found along the shore, under rocks or in pools left by the receding tide provided they are used for home consumption by the taker and not sold.

Maryland: **Blue Crab**

A license is not required. A person may not catch hard-shell crabs in any of the waters of the state between January 1 and April 1.

Hard Crabs, Peelers or Soft Crabs

A person may not catch or possess more than four hard crabs per bushel which measures less than five inches across the shell from tip to tip of spike, or any soft crabs measuring less than three and one-half inches across the shell from tip to tip of spike. Female egg-bearing crabs may not be taken and must be returned to the water. A person who does not possess a license to catch crabs **may not** catch more than one bushel of crabs on any one day.

Special Note

To catch more crabs than above described requires a state license. The laws regarding the methods and areas of crabbing are so voluminous that a copy should be requested from the Fisheries Administration of Maryland, in order to apprise the licensed crabber of the many specific rules and regulations involved.

Massachusetts: **Blue Crab**

A crab permit is required of all persons before they may catch edible crabs in coastal waters; however, no permit is required to take edible crabs for use by the immediate family (provided the number of crabs does not exceed fifty in one day and no **pots** or **traps** are used). Crab season is closed from December 1 to April 1. No minimum size or prohibition on egg-bearing females is stipulated.

Mississippi: **Blue Crab**

No license requirement is stipulated with the exception that if more than ten crab traps are used, a license is then required at a cost of $2.25. There is no set season on crabs and there is no size limit. Egg-bearing females may be taken except within one mile of Petit Bois, Horn and Ship Islands. No catch limit is specified as to the number of crabs that can be taken.

New Jersey: **Blue Crab**

No license or permit is required except for crab dredging. No person shall take any Crustacean, commonly known as crabs, from any of the tidal waters of this state, except Delaware Bay, by means of a line with more than ten baits attached thereto, under a penalty of twenty dollars for each offense. No person shall take or have in his possession a crab with eggs or spawns attached thereto, or from which the egg pouch or bunion has been removed. Under penalty of twenty dollars for each crab taken or possessed, no person shall take or have in his possession any peeler or shedder crab measuring less than three and one-half inches across the back from tip to tip of spike, or soft crab measuring less than three and one-half inches across the back from tip to tip of spike. There is no catch limit.

New York: **Blue Crab**

There is no license requirement. Egg-bearing females shall not be taken or possessed. A permit is required for commercial purposes.

North Carolina: **Blue Crab**

No license is required. An individual may take hard crabs through the use of crab pots at any time for personal consumption, provided not more than one crab pot is used and no boat is used to aid in the taking. Taking and possessing any hard crab measuring less than five inches from tip of spike to tip of spike is prohibited. Undersized crabs must be immediately returned to the waters from which they were taken. There is no catch limit and female egg-bearing crabs may be taken.

Rhode Island: **Blue Crab**

Residents only may crab. No license is required. There are no daily limits. The season for crabbing is from May 1 to November 30. Size limit shall not be less than four and one-eighth inches across shell from tip of spikes. Crabs can only be taken by scoop, crab net, trot or hand line. Egg-bearing females may not be taken but must be returned to the water.

South Carolina: **Blue Crab**

No license is required except if crab pots are used. The license fee is $10.00 per hundred; $50.00 for non-residents. The license fee for crab trotlines is $3.00 for each line. Any person, however, may set not more than two crab pots, with his name attached to the float for his personal benefit without obtaining a license. The size limit shall be no less than five inches measured from tip of point across the back of the shell. Egg-bearing females shall not be taken and must be returned to the water. A license is required for trawling.

Texas: **Blue Crab**

No license is required. Crabs may be taken in any number at any time and by any method except it is unlawful to take egg-bearing female crabs. There are, however, special provisions regarding certain areas marking buoys of crab traps and crab trawl sizes.

Virginia: **Blue Crab**

No license is required; however, a person may only take crabs with a hand line, dip net, or one single crab pot for family use. A license is required if taken by any other means or with more than one crab pot. For residents, license fees are:

1. Patent trot line $ 3.75
2. Crab pots   15.00
3. Power boat with power-lifted scrapes or dredges   30.00
4. Each crab trap or crab pound   each   3.00
5. Scraping crabs with hand scrape   8.25

The size limit is four and three-fourths inches across the shell from tip to tip of the longest spikes. All under-sized crabs must be immediately returned to the same waters.

"Sponge crabs" (female egg-bearing crabs) may not be taken or possessed from May 15 to September 15 (both dates included) of every year. Certain areas are exempted from this provision (see laws of Virginia relating to fisheries of tidal waters with supplement). The catch limit is one bushel of crabs per day.

State laws do sometimes change from year to year, so if you should desire to obtain a copy of the local state laws concerning crabbing, you may direct your request to the following agencies:

Alabama:

State of Alabama Department of Conservation
and Natural Resources
Post Office Box 188
Dauphin Island, Alabama 36528

Connecticut:

State of Connecticut Department
of Environmental Protection
State Office Building
Hartford, Connecticut 06115

Delaware:

State of Delaware Department of Natural Resources
and Environmental Control
Dover, Delaware 19901

Florida:

State of Florida Department
of Natural Resources
Tallahassee, Florida 32304

Georgia:

State of Georgia Department
of Natural Resources

270 Washington St. S.W.
Atlanta, Georgia 30334

Louisiana:
Louisiana Wild Life and
Fisheries Commission
126 Wildlife and Fisheries Building
400 Royal Street
New Orleans, Louisiana 70130

Maine:
State of Maine Department
of Marine Resources
State House Annex
Capitol Shopping Center
Augusta, Maine 04333

Maryland:
State of Maryland
Fisheries Administration
Dawes Building
500 Taylor Avenue
Building B, Second Floor
Annapolis, Maryland 21401

Massachusetts:
State of Massachusetts
Department of Natural Resources
Division of Marine Fisheries
Leverett Saltonstall Building
100 Cambridge Street (Government Center)
Boston, Massachusetts 02202

Mississippi:
Mississippi Marine Conservation Commission
1201 East Bayview
Biloxi, Mississippi 39530

New Jersey:
State of New Jersey
Department of Environmental Protection
Division of Fish, Game and Shell Fisheries
P.O. Box 1809
Trenton, New Jersey 08625

New York:
New York Department of
Environmental Conservation
Building 40
State University of New York
Stony Brook, New York 11795

North Carolina:
North Carolina Department of Natural
and Economic Resources
Post Office Box 27687
Raleigh, North Carolina 27611

Rhode Island:
State of Rhode Island and Providence Plantations
Department of Natural Resources (Division of Wildlife)
83 Park Street
Providence, Rhode Island 02903

South Carolina:
South Carolina Wildlife Resources Department
Marine Resources Division
Post Office Box 12559
Charleston, South Carolina 29412

Texas:
State of Texas Parks and Wildlife Department
John F. Reagan State Office Building
Austin, Texas 78701

Virginia:
Commonwealth of Virginia
 Marine Resources Commission
Post Office Box 756
2401 West Avenue
Newport News, Virginia 23607

CHAPTER 9

EDIBLE CRABS — WEST COAST
STATE LAWS AND REGULATIONS

The blue claw crab and the stone crab, located and found along the Atlantic and Gulf Coast states, are not indigenous to the Pacific Coast states; rather, the edible crabs of the Pacific shores and waters are specifically the Dungeness crab, red or rock crab, and the Alaskan king crab (sometimes called the Japanese crab).

The Pacific Coast states, California, Oregon, Washington and Alaska also have laws regulating their fish and wildlife resources and it is advisable that the crabber familiarize himself with the local state statutes when and if he crabs in these waters. The following synopsis of these state laws is published for information and as a guide to the individual sportsman. A point to note is, that at the present time, there are no regulations, laws or restrictions in the taking or catching of the red or rock crab in any of the four states. Also, because the Alaskan king crab is taken commercially and not generally by the sportsman, no regulations relating to the king crab will be discussed in this chapter.

PRESENT LAWS

(Alphabetical Order)

Alaska: **The Dungeness Crab**
No license is required. Under Alaska regulations, only hard-shell Dungeness male crabs over six and one-half inches in shell width may be taken (see one exception). The sport catch limit is thirty crabs per day (see one exception). Spears and gaffs are not permitted in the Ketchikan and Sitka districts (Districts 1 and 2). A license is required for pots or other gear, not including hand lines, rings or hand or dip nets. There are, however, open and closed seasons throughout Alaska to wit:

48

1. Port Federick is closed to all Dungeness crab fishing.
2. Dungeness crabs may be taken or possessed in southern Alaska — Yakutat from May 16 through March 31 with the following exceptions:
   (a) **District 5:** Closed from April 1 through June 30 between latitude of Boulder Point and the Latitude of Summit Island.
   (b) **District 6:** Closed from April 1 through July 30 North of latitude of Point Baker Light, excluding Urangeli Narrows north to Burnt Island.
3. **Prince William Sound:**
   There is no closed season for Dungeness crabs except that north of 60⁰, 24 minutes North Latitude and south of a line from Johnstone Point to Sheep Point, Dungeness crabs may be taken only from 12: 01 p.m. August 31 until 12: 01 p.m. June 1.
4. **Cook Inlet:**
   There is no closed season on Dungeness crabs except that in Katchemak Bay northeast of a line extending from Coal Point to the northeast tip of Glacier Spit, Dungeness crabs may not be taken from May 1 through August 31.
5. **Kodiak District:**
   There is no closed season on Dungeness crabs except that in the waters of the Kodiak District south of latitude of Boot Point and south of latitude of Cape Ikolik, Dungeness crabs may only be taken from June 15 through April 30. In the Kodiak and Chignik Districts, no male Dungeness crabs may be taken or possessed that are less than seven inches in shoulder width.

California: The Dungeness Crab

A license is required of both residents and non-residents. The fee for residents is four dollars; for non-residents, it is fifteen dollars. All crustaceans taken under the authority of a sport fishing license may not be sold, exchanged or bartered. The minimum size is six and one-fourth inches measured by the shortest distance through the body from edge of shell to edge of shell directly in front of and excluding the points (lateral spines). Every person while taking invertebrates which have size limits shall carry a device which is capable of accurately measuring the size of the species taken. The open seasons are as follows: (1) Del Norte, Humbolt and Mendocino counties: December 1 through July 30. All other counties: the second Tuesday in November through June 30.

Catch limit is ten per day. The gear restrictions are (general): no nets, traps, or other appliances may be used to take salt water crustaceans except baited hoop nets (rings). Crab traps shall have at least two rigid circular openings of not less than four inches inside diameter so constructed that the lowest portion of each opening is no lower than five inches from the top of the trap. Crab trap areas: Crab traps may be used north of Port Arguello to take all species of crabs. Diving for crustaceans is permissable, but divers may take crustaceans only by the use of hands. No hook device may be used.

Oregon: **The Dungeness Crab**
No license is required. Only male crabs may be taken, and the minimum size is five and one-half inches across the back, exclusive of spines. No more than twenty four may be taken in any 7 consecutive days. Dungeness crabs may be taken by the use of crab rings or pots, not to exceed 3 in combination per person. Crabs may also be taken by hand, dip net, rake or baited lines. Bays and ocean beaches are open all year. The Pacific Ocean is closed from August 16 through November 30. It is unlawful to back or disfigure crabs in any manner prior to landing. Undersized or female crabs must be returned to the water in a manner which will not cause injury.

Washington: **The Dungeness Crab**
No license requirement exists. There is open season during the entire year. Bag limit is six male crabs with the minimum size being not less than six inches across the back measured in a horizontal line immediately in front of the points. Possession of female, soft-shell crabs or undersized crabs is prohibited. Legal fishing gear includes one ring net or two crab pots; or crabs may be taken by hand or with any hand-operated instrument which will not penetrate the shell. The name and address of the owner must be placed on the marker buoy when crab pots or ring nets are left unattended. Crab pots must be covered by water at all times. It is unlawful to possess a crab in the field from which the back has been removed. It is unlawful to fish (crab) with a spear or other instrument that penetrates the crab shell. It shall be unlawful to possess crabs which have been caught with trawl, seine, weir, gill or similar net gear.

State laws may change from time to time. If anyone wishes a

copy of any of the Pacific Coast State Laws, requests should be directed to the following:

Alaska:
Alaska Department of Fishing and Game
Sub Port Building
Juneau, Alaska 99801

California:
State of California Resource Agency
Department of Fishing and Game
1416 Ninth Street
Sacramento, California 95814

Oregon:
Oregon State Wildlife Commission
1634 West Alder Street
Post Office Box 3503
Portland, Oregon 97208

Washington:
State of Washington Department of Fisheries
Room 115
General Administration Building
Olympia, Washington 98504

CHAPTER 10

SUMMARY

When armed with the knowledge presented in the preceding chapters, the capture of this popular table crustacean should be easy and most successful. But how is this wealth of information utilized to advantage? Obviously, only by proper analysis and evaluation of a situation or problem can this knowledge be of any real value to the crabber. A mental reasoning process must take place in order to culminate in the solution of the problem at hand. Perhaps the best and easiest way to explain this mental evaluation and elimination process is to list a number of hypothetical premises (propositions) and then discuss each in simple order, step by step. In this way, the crabber will develop the idea, become familiar with and understand what is involved and, as a result, be able to intelligently solve any condition or situation that may arise when venturing out to catch this sometimes elusive adversary. However, it is extremely important that all facts be taken into consideration including the time of year, season, area location, weather, tides and the applicable state laws.

Premise 1:

It is February and you wish to go crabbing somewhere in the waters of New Jersey. Would you be likely to catch any crabs?

Reasoning and Analysis:

In most East Coast states (New Jersey included), the blue claw crab goes into the mud in October and November and then hibernates during the winter (see Chapter 2; also Figures 1, 2, 3). The blue claw crab does not emerge again or become active until the spring. Therefore, February, being a winter month, the crabs would be hibernating and could not be caught by any means except by dredging. (A license for this is necessary in New Jersey (see Chapter 8).

Answer:

No. Crabs would not be caught at this time except by dredging. This answer would apply to all East Coast states from Maine to Georgia.

Premise 2:
It is July and you wish to go crabbing in Maryland. Would you go to the saltier waters in the lower bays or would you crab in the less salty waters of the upper bays and estuaries?

Reasoning and Analysis:
The mating season of the blue claw crab generally begins in May and continues into October (see Chapter 4). The adult female seeks out a mature male who normally is in fresher (brackish) waters in the upper bays and nearer the river mouths. July is a mating month and therefore, most adult crabs would be found (both male and female) in the less saltier waters.

Answer:
You would go where most crabs are located at this time of the year, namely the upper bay and river estuaries. This applies to all states along the Eastern Seaboard.

Premise 3:
It is late October in North Carolina and you are crabbing in the lower waters near the ocean. Would you be catching more male crabs, more female crabs or an equal amount of each?

Reasoning and Analysis:
By fall, most adult females have mated and, due to their life cycle (see Chapter 2), they begin to migrate or have migrated to the saltier waters nearer the ocean (see Chapter 4). Male crabs do not accompany the females but tend to remain in the upper and middle bays. Because of this normal and usual cycle, it is evident that most crabs found near the ocean would be female crabs.

Answer:
You would be catching more and mostly female crabs. These crabs would be sponge crabs, but in North Carolina they may be taken, as there is no law prohibiting the taking of egg-bearing crabs.

Premise 4:
It is August 30 and you wish to crab in Oregon in the shallow off-shore waters of the Pacific Ocean. Could you legally do this?

Reasoning and Analysis:
Oregon has no closed season for crabbing the bays and ocean beaches; however, the Pacific off-shore waters are closed to Dungeness crabbing from August 16 through November 30 (see Chapter 9). August 30 is within the

closed season and, therefore, the sportsman may not take Dungeness crabs from the Pacific Ocean at this time. There are, however, no laws relating to red or rock crabs and it follows that you could crab for red or rock crabs anytime, anywhere.

Answer:

Yes. You could crab in this area at this time but only for red or rock crabs.

Premise 5:

During December, in the state of Louisiana, you have just caught a hard-shell female blue claw crab (not egg-bearing) that measures 4 inches from tip of spike to tip of spike. Can you keep this crab or must you return it to the water?

Reasoning and Analysis:

Here we are dealing with the state law and must refer to its limitations and prohibitions if any (see Chapter 8). The law states that (1) there is no set season so it is legal to crab during December; (2) Egg-bearing females must be returned to the water, but since this particular crab, even though not egg-bearing, is only four inches in width, it would be illegal to take her; (3) minimum size for any hard-shell crab is five inches in width.

Answer:

You must return this crab to the water as it is under legal minimum size.

Premise 6:

In the state of Washington you have just caught a "Doubler" (male with a soft-shelled female underneath) Dungeness crab. The size of the male is six and one-half inches; the size of the female is five inches. Can you keep one, both, or must both be returned to the water?

Reasoning and Analysis:

Again in this case, state law governs (see Chapter 9). In the State of Washington you can only take male Dungness crabs; therefore, the female must be returned to the water. The possession of soft-shell crabs is also prohibited. The minimum size for hard-shell Dungeness crabs is six inches. The hard-shell male in Premise 6 is six and one-half inches so it may be taken.

Answer:

You may keep one crab, the hard-shell male Dungeness.

After studying the premises mentioned, a solid foundation in reasoning with knowledge should be established and understood. The facts you have learned are not only interesting, but are valuable in the catching of edible crabs. However, more information is necessary in order to become an expert crabber. Part II will explain and discuss the various techniques and methods used in catching crabs. It will also describe the effects of weather, tides, various water conditions and bottom locations which, of course, are most important to know.

PART II
CRABBING METHODS AND TECHNIQUES

CHAPTER 1

GENERAL EXPLANATION

Crabbing is a simple, easy to learn, most exciting, full-of-fun sport. Basically, it is a sport for everyone and anyone who is not overly squeamish or afraid to look at, be near, catch, or handle a live, strange and ferocious looking, crawling, snapping, aggressive little animal. Most apprehensions felt by the crabber are caused by inexperience and a lack of fundamental knowledge. They may also be present when a crabber feels he cannot handle this active, quick -moving creature properly. Anyone who is foolish enough to put a bare hand into a basket full of live hard -shell crabs will surely be bitten — and How! Soft -shell crabs do not have the ability to bite. You can learn from Figures 1, 2 and 3 how to handle a live, moving hard -shell crab with your bare hands. Your apprehensions should vanish and your self-confidence be completely restored. However, if you do not find this adequately reassuring, you will need some heavy commercial rubber gloves or wooden or metal tongs to pick up this "fighting for his life" crab.

You will note when viewing the diagram (Figure 2) that a crab must be held in the rear, away from the snapping claws. You must hold him still by lightly pressing on the top shell with a shoe, stick, long screwdriver, or other apparatus (see Figure 1). Too much pressure will crack the shell. The thumb should then be placed on top of the swimming paddle where it meets the body (shell) and the forefinger placed underneath where the same swimming paddle meets the underbody. When the crab is held tightly, you can then pick him up without being bitten. It is not possible for the crab to reach back this far and bite the fingers because of his body conformation. If the crab is held in this manner, using thumb and forefinger with other fingers closed into the palm of the hand (see Figure 3), the crabber is safe. Either thumb and forefinger (left or right hand), or both, may be used to pick up, look at, or transport a crab.

When crabs are caught, they should be placed into some sort of receptacle for holding and keeping. The best container is a wooden bushel basket (obtainable at any fruit or vegetable store). A 50 pound or a 100 pound potato or onion sack (burlap bag or onion bag) without holes serves as an excellent and convenient receptacle for holding crabs. A pail or bucket, whether metal or plastic, is not advisable for the purpose of confining a crab catch because air cannot flow through this

57

type of container. Usually the crabs will die before you reach home (see Part III, Chapter 1). It is not recommended that crabs be placed in a pail or bucket containing water unless the water is replenished or changed often. The oxygen in the water is soon exhausted and all of the crabs will expire. Storage containers should be kept out of the hot sun. If this is not possible, they should be covered with a wet rag, shirt, towel or some other light cover to keep the sun rays from beating down on your catch. Occasional "wetting down" the crabs thus held will extend their lives until you reach your destination. This may be done by dipping the container into the water from time to time or by pouring water directly over the crabs. Blue claw, dungeness, and red or rock crabs can live out of water for extended periods of time if properly handled and if these precautionary methods are used (see Part I, Chapter 1). A bushel basket full of hard-shell blue claw crabs weighs approximately 35 pounds and contains between 90 and 120 legal size crabs, depending upon the size of the crabs.

When you catch a "Doubler"(male with female underneath), do not put this female ("buster" or soft-shell) into the same receptacle with the hard -shell crabs, as they will either eat or kill this crab. Instead, separate these soft crabs and place them in another container. Later, upon arriving home, you will enjoy a real treat by dining on these delicious fried soft -shell crabs (see Part III).

It is very important to know the local state laws when crabbing, as set forth in Part I, Chapters 8 and 9. A ruler or calipers should be part of your crabbing equipment so there can be no mistake as to which crabs are legal "keepers" and which must be returned to the waters. The crabber must also be able to distinguish a male, a female and an egg- bearing female (see Part I, Chapter 4, Figure 1-A, B and C).

Crabbing can be done from many places and in many areas such as docks, piers, bulkheads, bridges, from shore, in the water or from a boat. Crabs can sometimes be caught in abundance from any of these places depending upon existing circumstances and the situation at hand however, certain equipment, methods and techniques must be employed in lieu of others because of the location and varied conditions. All methods will be explained fully in subsequent chapters to enable the crabber to decide which is best for each of his crabbing expeditions.

It is important to know the depth of water, the wind velocity, the weather, the current temperatures and types of bottoms when using the different types of crabbing gear. Knowledge of natural elements must be considered when deciding where and when you will crab, as well as what equipment you will use and how it may be used most effectively. Believe it or not, this information, properly utilized, can make the difference between a fine day's catch of crabs and being "skunked" (no catch).

The various types of crabbing methods and techniques will be discussed and explained in detail in Part II. All of the equipment mentioned can be purchased in many sporting shops or can easily be made by the crabber himself.

Baits and chumming will be covered in Part II (Chapter 3).

The most important ingredient of any crabbing experience is a simple word: PATIENCE. It is a definite MUST word; yes, a real virtue. Take your time and don't RUSH the capture when using a line. **E A S Y** does it! Experience is naturally the best teacher, so go forth, my hearties, and try crabbing. You may have the time of your life!

FIGURE 1

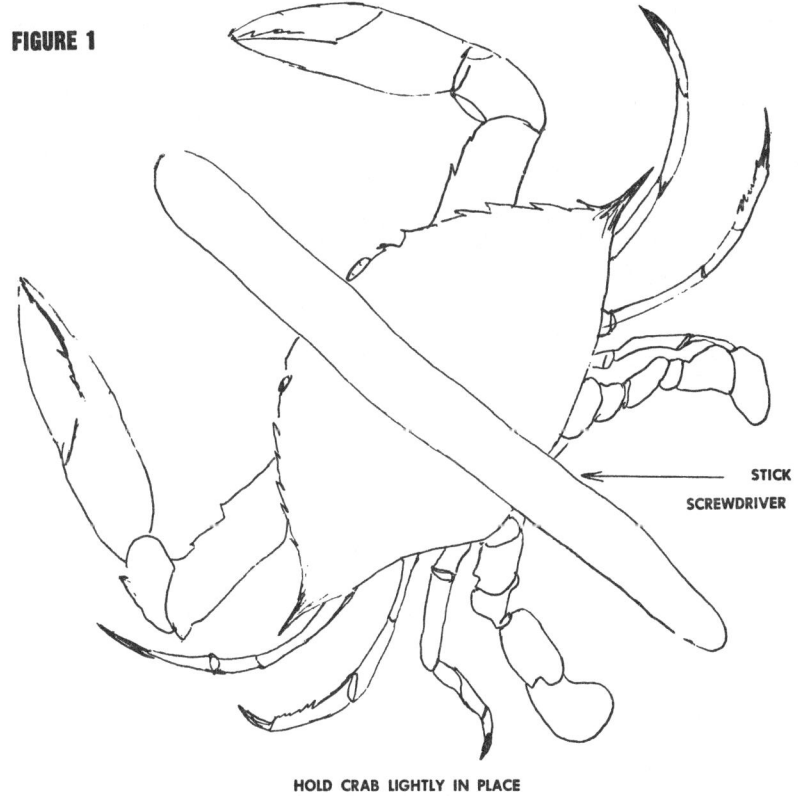

STICK
SCREWDRIVER

HOLD CRAB LIGHTLY IN PLACE
WITH SHOE, STICK OR OTHER
APPARATUS AVAILABLE.

HOW TO HANDLE LIVE HARD SHELL CRAB WITH BARE HANDS

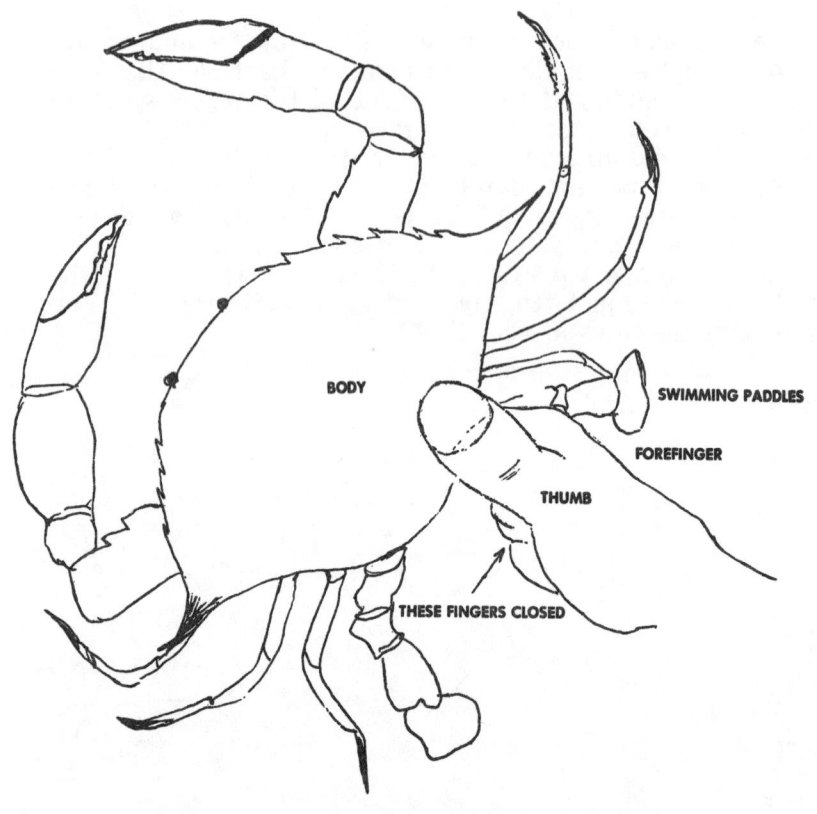

BODY

SWIMMING PADDLES

FOREFINGER

THUMB

THESE FINGERS CLOSED

FIGURE 2   HOW TO HANDLE LIVE HARD SHELL CRAB WITH BARE HANDS

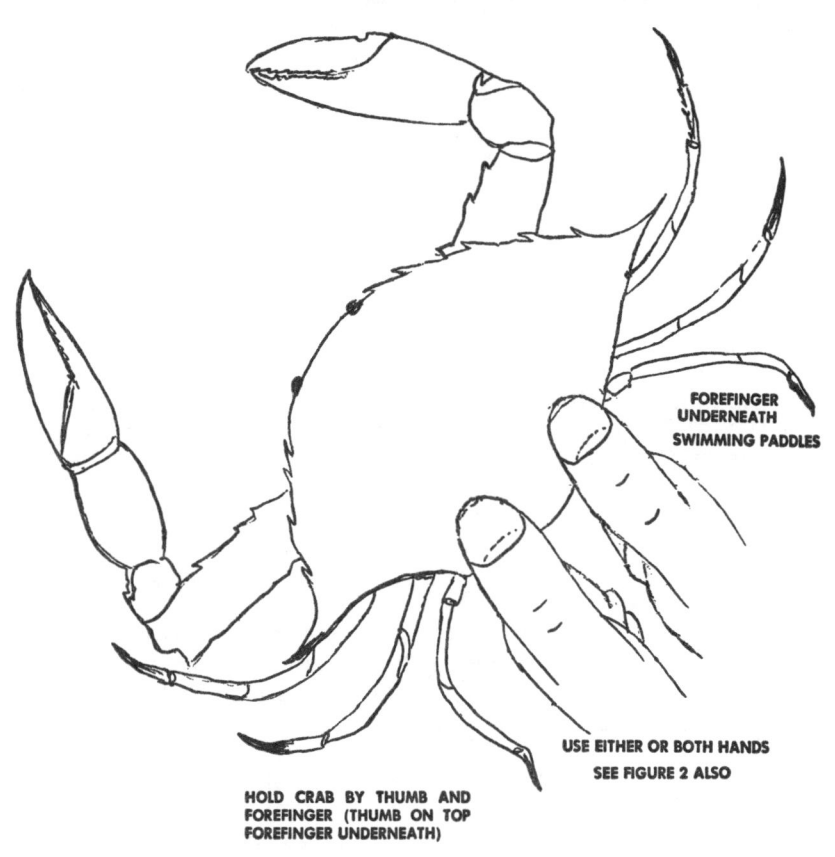

FOREFINGER
UNDERNEATH

SWIMMING PADDLES

USE EITHER OR BOTH HANDS

SEE FIGURE 2 ALSO

HOLD CRAB BY THUMB AND
FOREFINGER (THUMB ON TOP
FOREFINGER UNDERNEATH)

FIGURE 3   HOW TO HANDLE A LIVE HARD SHELL CRAB WITH BARE HANDS

CHAPTER 2

HAND LINES, WEIGHTS AND BAITS

The most common and most frequently practiced method for catching crabs is the use and application of hand lines (weights and baits). This particular method is by far the most challenging, exciting, enjoyable, suspenseful and fun-providing of all. It can also be, at times, the most frustrating method, but the ardent crabber will find it very satisfying in accomplishment. It not only puts the sportsman in "fingertip touch" with his unseen prey, but also strongly tests his current and potential abilities to the infinite in patience, knowledge, coordination, restraint and endurance. It is a real "live" contest between man and animal and a most fascinating participating sport. This method of crabbing is so remarkable that **anyone,** male, female, young or old, can partake and, with a little knowledge and practice, become an amazingly proficient crabber in no time at all. Even more surprising is the fact that this method can be employed at little or no cost to the participant. It requires only a length of string, cord or even rope, a weight of some sort (a sinker, 1, 2, or 3 ounce type used in fishing) an old bolt, an old door hinge or an old small lock without the key, some kind of bait (fish, fishheads, trimmings, see Part I, Chapter 5) from the local meat market, and a scoop or dip net which may be hand-made, borrowed or purchased. Any of these items can be quickly obtained at home, from a neighbor, or from the local shopkeeper. Not much to it, is there? A good strong cord, either butcher's cord or nylon cord, is preferable. This can be purchased by the ball, but any type of strong line will do. A large four-inch electric metal clamp, obtainable at any electric supply store, is an excellent piece of equipment to have since it serves a dual purpose. It not only acts as a holder for the bait, but is heavy enough to use as a weight. This is accomplished by opening the jaws of the clamp, inserting the bait and allowing the clamp to close tightly on the bait. The bait will float and will not reach bottom where the crabs generally roam if you do not have a weight on your line. These items must all be put together (see Figure 1) when preparing to crab. First, make certain the cord is long enough to reach the bottom where you intend to crab. It is always wise to have a little extra line so that it is not too taut but has a little bottom play. It is also necessary to allow enough line for securing the upper end to a permanent object (see Figure 2).

Next, tie the weight on tightly by using simple overhand knots about a foot from one end of the cord. The bait should then be tied near or around (but not above) the weight by using the rest of the cord that is between the weight and short end in a similar manner. The bait must be tied tightly. Lastly, cut off the short dangling end, if any (Figure 1 shows step-by-step instructions and how the completed line will look).

The line, weight and bait method can be used in a multitude of places (see Figure 2-A, docks; 2-B, shore; 2-C, in the water; and 2-D, from a boat). You can make up as many lines as you wish to use and which you can conveniently handle. Normally, this depends upon the area or location in which you are crabbing. This is your choice. Too many lines close together have a tendency to get entangled with each other. This is no fun because it involves extra time and work to untangle these lines. You must use your own judgment in this regard. One important consideration to remember is that the use of hand lines is restricted to the length of your scoop or dip net and the height (distance) you are from the water; if, for example, you are on a high twenty-foot bridge, you could not possibly reach down to scoop up the crab at the end of your line. In this case, another method would have to be used (see subsequent chapters 4, 5 and 7). **You must be able to reach the water with your net.**

When your hand lines are ready for use and you have dropped or thrown them into the water and they are firmly on the bottom and secured on top, you must wait a while for the crabs to be attracted by the bait. It is presumed, of course, that you applied the knowledge obtained in Part I when you selected your crabbing location. After a short wait, a few minutes or so, lightly pick up the line by means of thumb and forefinger. This gives you a more delicate feel and enables you to see if a crab has been attracted to and is eating your bait. You will know if a crab is on your line, as the pulling and clawing action will be transmitted up the line to your finger tips. If he is on your line, then slowly, using thumb and forefinger, hand-over-hand, inch by inch (left hand, thumb and forefinger, then right hand, thumb and forefinger). Your line should be gently eased upward. This procedure is important because the crab does not know or feel he is being lifted to the surface. He is normally so busy eating that he is unaware he is being elevated from the bottom. Do not pull the line too fast or use jerky movements because this will scare him off. If he does drop off the line, return it to the water and wait. Great patience and much time are required when bringing your line to the surface in this manner, depending upon how much line is out (line distance of six, ten, fifteen feet, or how much you happen to need at your particular location). Keep the line tight with the crab on one end and you on the other. When you can see the crab near the surface, get your net (see Figure 3) ready with one hand and hold the line with the other, using thumb and forefinger. The crab must then be maneuvered in as close as possible in order to reach him with the net. Quickly, and at the time you consider the precise moment for action, scoop down alongside and under the crab and then up with a wrist-turning motion. The crab, bait, line and sinker will then be in the net. Do not dig into the water too deep to get the crab. Stay as close to the surface as possible if you can.

You may miss netting a few crabs at first but don't be discouraged. This is the price of learning. Soon your judgment of distance, reflexes and coordination will become automatic and second-nature. You will surprise yourself with your new found dexterity and abilities. Of course, you can have a helper (one person to pull in the line and one person to do the netting (scooping). This is known as "team action." You will get the "hang" of this method within a short time and undoubtedly become an expert crabber.

After you have netted your crab, transfer him to your receptacle for holding (see and note information in previous chapter about keeping the container in shade or covered and wetting down the crabs). This is done by turning the net over (open end to receptacle) and shaking it a little to make him drop into the container. Sometimes the crab will hold on to the netting with his claws and it will take a lot of shaking to break him loose. You might even have to pull him out by hand (see Part II, Chapter 1).

The line, weight and bait method of crabbing works well when the surface water is fairly calm and the water reasonably clear. You must see the crab in order to net him. If the water is very murky and the surface choppy, this method should not be used, as the results will be very disheartening. You will get lots of bites; you will slowly pull him to the top, but the choppy water will scare him and you will lose him before he becomes visible. If this happens, use a trap, pot or seine. Also, if the tide is running fast, you must use a heavier weight to keep bait from floating or moving around on the bottom, as the turbulence may frighten the crab. So, you see, weather, wind and tides do affect the decision you make when deciding to crab. Take all these facts into consideration:

(1) Observe what other crabbers are doing, what methods they are using, and if they are catching any crabs.
(2) Don't be afraid to ask questions.

(3) Check and ask local people about crabbing and crabbing spots.

(4) Since each bit of information is valuable, make sure you have all you can get.

The above pointers will be very helpful to the crabber.

The author of this book has composed the following poem specifically for crabbers as an aid and review of the techniques involved in the use of hand lines (weights and baits):

THE ART OF CRABBING

Crabbing is a sport that offers lots of fun;
What's more, it can be done by almost anyone.
So drop in **your** line, tied with weight and bait,
Let it reach bottom, then relax and wait!
It's just as simple as can be
And I'm sure you'll agree with me!
In a little while, five minutes at best,
Check your line, you may have a guest.
If a hungry crab is on, you will surely know;
He will be pulling hard, so you pull up, but slow!
Don't forget, it's hand-over-hand and inch by inch,
The virtue of controlled patience makes it a cinch.
Up, up, slowly, slowly, patience must reign;
If the crab gets scared, drops off, then try again.
Most likely, he will return to eat once more,
So please pull up more slowly than before!
Ah, he's back eating again, you're doing great — don't stop
You have to get him closer, closer to the top.
There he is! You can plainly see him now!
A big one! A beauty! Oh, my — Oh, Wow!

The next step is to get ready with net,
Maneuver the crab in range; get set!
Now scoop! Down under the crab and up, **be quick**
What counts is the wrist action; that's the trick.
However, if you miss him, don't feel too much remorse
For scooping action takes a little practice, of course.

After a time or two, you will see
That scooping comes rather naturally.
Transferring a crab from net to basket you must know;
Just turn the net over, shake a little; he'll let go.
Remember, keep this basket in the shade
Or covered and wet down with water too;
This is the way they'll stay alive for you!
And when your basket is full, you can't help but say
"NOW I'M A CRABBER! WHAT A WONDERFUL DAY!"

ITEMS

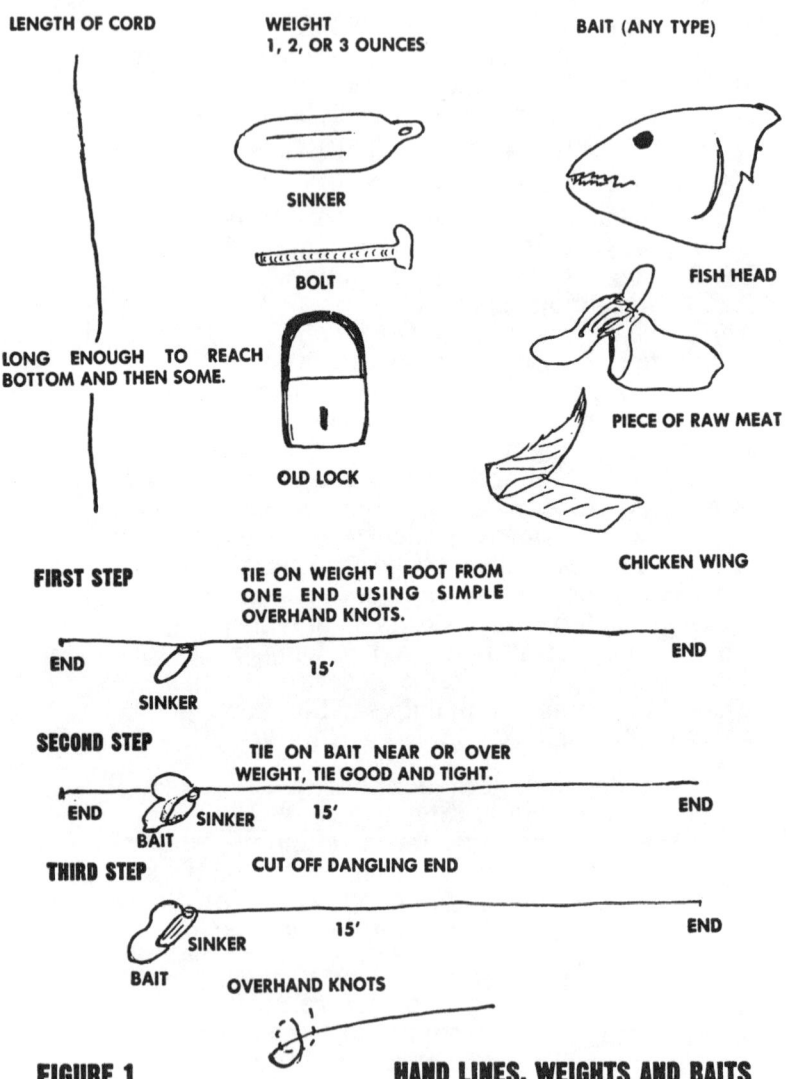

LENGTH OF CORD

WEIGHT
1, 2, OR 3 OUNCES

BAIT (ANY TYPE)

SINKER

BOLT

FISH HEAD

LONG ENOUGH TO REACH
BOTTOM AND THEN SOME.

PIECE OF RAW MEAT

OLD LOCK

CHICKEN WING

FIRST STEP   TIE ON WEIGHT 1 FOOT FROM
ONE END USING SIMPLE
OVERHAND KNOTS.

END   15'   END

SINKER

SECOND STEP   TIE ON BAIT NEAR OR OVER
WEIGHT, TIE GOOD AND TIGHT.

END   SINKER   15'   END

BAIT

THIRD STEP   CUT OFF DANGLING END

SINKER   15'   END

BAIT   OVERHAND KNOTS

FIGURE 1   **HAND LINES, WEIGHTS AND BAITS**

A. DOCK

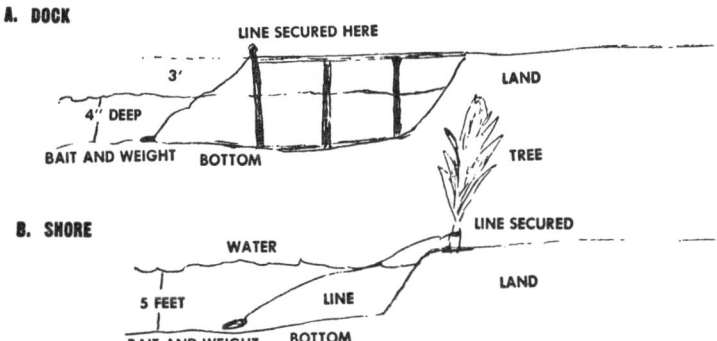

LINE SECURED HERE

3'

4" DEEP

LAND

BAIT AND WEIGHT   BOTTOM

B. SHORE

TREE

WATER

LINE SECURED

LAND

5 FEET   LINE

BAIT AND WEIGHT   BOTTOM

C. IN WATER

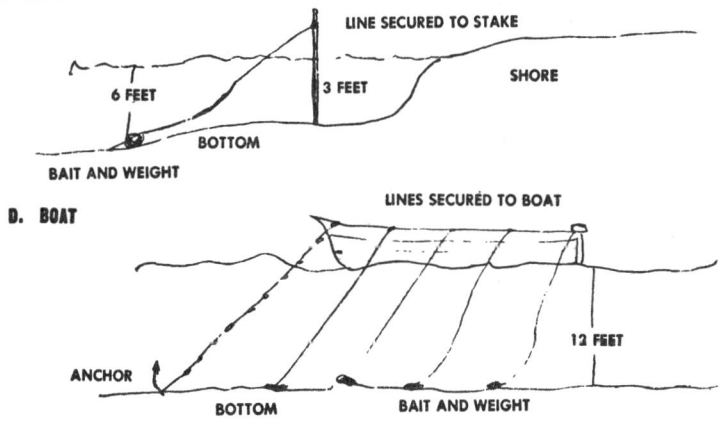

STAKE DRIVEN INTO BOTTOM

LINE SECURED TO STAKE

6 FEET   3 FEET

SHORE

BOTTOM

BAIT AND WEIGHT

D. BOAT

LINES SECURED TO BOAT

12 FEET

ANCHOR

BOTTOM   BAIT AND WEIGHT

FIGURE 2   **HANDLINES, WEIGHTS AND BAITS**

67

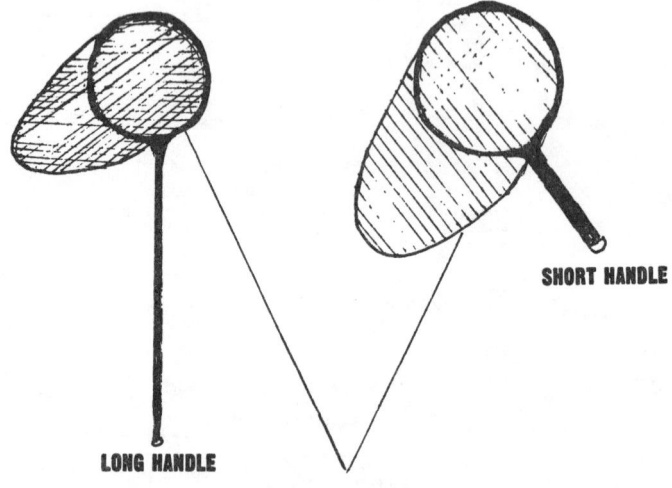

SHORT HANDLE

LONG HANDLE

VARIOUS OPENING DIAMETERS

SCOOP OR DIP NETS COME IN
VARIOUS SIZES AND LENGTHS

(SEE PART II, CHAPTER 7)

FIGURE 3   **SCOOP OR DIP NET**

CHAPTER 3

TYPES OF BAITS

The selection of a bait that will attract and catch crabs should present little or no problem to the crabber. A wide variety of common baits was listed in Part I, Chapter 5. They are all good and are used by crabbers on both coasts. Which one should you use? A good "rule of thumb" to follow is: (1) Use the bait or baits you prefer or can easily handle; (2) Use bait that is readily available or plentiful; and (3) Use the least expensive bait or that which can be obtained at no cost. Your own good judgement and accumulative experience will eventually dictate which are your favorites or which baits have preference over others. Your choice will be conclusive when you have experimented with all baits. An adequate supply of bait should be on hand when you go crabbing. Crabs, when they are "biting," consume the bait rapidly. You will be surprised how fast crabs can strip a fish to the bone. It is an "unforgivable sin" to have to stop crabbing just when they are eating your bait because your supply has been depleted. Shame! If, on the other hand, you have some unused bait left at the end of your crabbing day, you can either take it home and freeze it or it may be saved for your next crabbing outing. You may also throw the bait into the water and bestow a free or "bonus" meal to the hungry, uncaught crabs; or, if you feel charitable, you may offer it to your fellow crabbers.

Lifeless fish, fresh or frozen (any kind) is the most popular natural bait and undoubtedly the most widely used. Fish can generally be obtained quite easily. They can be caught or purchased and the trimmings (head, bodies and parts) can be procured from a fish market at little or no cost. When using a hand line or lines, it is not necessary to tie on a whole fish. If you have whole fish on hand, cut them into parts. Your bait will then last longer if parts are used. It is best to use a whole fish (or several) when using a trap or crab pot, as this equipment is not brought to the surface as often as hand lines (see Part II, Chapter 4). Crabs seem to be attracted more by oily fish than those containing less oil. Crabs are constantly roaming the bottom and will find your bait sooner or later, whatever it may be. Crabs are always in search of edible food so, again, be patient. Perhaps you may facilitate their arrival and keep them in your area longer by using a chum pot or chum bag, commonly known as "chumming" (see Figure 1). Chum is finely ground fish that looks like baby food. The chum is placed into a can, preferably a coffee can with a plastic top. Place the top on the can and with the sharp point of a knife, punch lots of holes into the can. This will allow chum to filter slowly into the surrounding water. A cord is then tied through one of the holes and the can may then be lowered to the bottom. The other end of the cord should be tied securely to some fixed and permanent object. Chuming is generally used when crabbing from a boat. The cord must be pulled up and down every now and then for the purpose of shaking the contents and allowing the chum to flow out of the holes. A plastic piece of screening or cheese cloth-type material may be used to make a "chum bag." The chum should be placed inside a piece of the material you have elected to use. This material should be one to one and one-half feet square. The four ends are then gathered up and tied together tightly with a cord to which a weight has been attached. This will allow the bag to go to the bottom or near-bottom. Again, the cord must occasionally be pulled up and down to shake the chum (see Figure 2).

Live-fish, such as killies, spearing, herring and other small fish, can be strung on a wire such as a coat hanger or piano wire (leader) and then formed into a circle. Each fish is strung by putting the wire in and through one gill and the mouth (see Figure 3). This method is used with hand lines and works very well. Crabbing may then proceed as explained in Part II, Chapter 2.

Eels, fresh frozen and preserved (salted down in brine) are excellent bait. They hold up well and are not eaten as rapidly as most fish because their skin is extremely tough. It takes a long time for crabs to completely devour a piece of eel. Eel baits are normally used with hand lines and trotlines and may be used over and over on several crabbing outings if saved and salted down in brine.

Squid is a very good bait; however, it is soft and will be quickly consumed. Consequently, it must be replaced often. Squid may be purchased at most supermarkets in one and three-pound packages (frozen.) The present approximate price is sixty cents a pound. Unused squid can be refrozen and stored in the freezer for the next crabbing trip.

Meat trimmings, meats of all kinds, make fine baits. Crabs usually enjoy meat and inner organs of all animals. A visit to your butcher or meat market will undoubtedly result in a "bag full of scraps" at little or no cost to you. You should be sure there is some meat on the trimmings because ALL FAT is not too popular with crabs.

Chicken backs or necks are not only good crabbing baits but can be readily obtained. They last longer than most fish and are very inexpensive (approximately twenty-nine cents a pound). Chicken backs and necks are the only baits used by some crabbers because they are easy to handle and tie to the cord; also, they are not quite as "messy" as fish to use.

Clams (out of shell) are fine for baiting and chumming. Unless you get them at no cost or dig them yourself though, they are quite expensive and unprofitable to use as bait.

Don't use too heavy a piece of bait when using a hand line. It reduces the touch, feel and sensitivity, and may even prevent you from knowing when a crab is on your line.

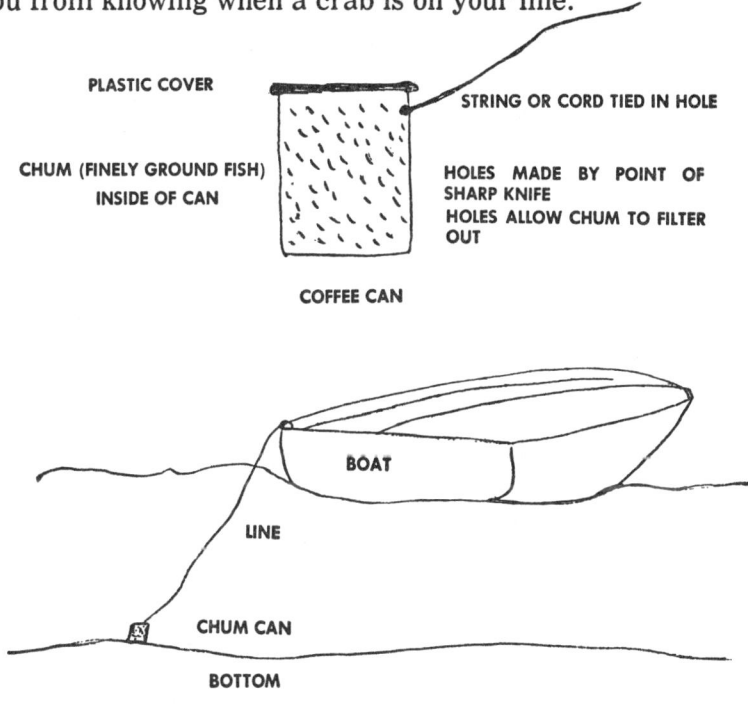

PLASTIC COVER

STRING OR CORD TIED IN HOLE

CHUM (FINELY GROUND FISH) INSIDE OF CAN

HOLES MADE BY POINT OF SHARP KNIFE
HOLES ALLOW CHUM TO FILTER OUT

COFFEE CAN

BOAT

LINE

CHUM CAN

BOTTOM

FIGURE 1   **CHUMMING CAN**

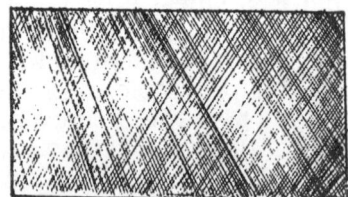

1 ½′

1 TO 1 ½ FEET SQUARE PIECE OF
PLASTIC SCREENING OR CHEESE
CLOTH (LOOSELY KNITTED
MATERIAL)

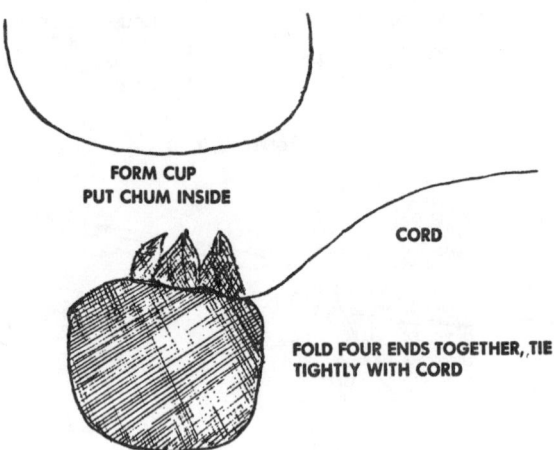

FORM CUP
PUT CHUM INSIDE

CORD

FOLD FOUR ENDS TOGETHER, TIE
TIGHTLY WITH CORD

FIGURE 2   **CHUMMING SCREEN**

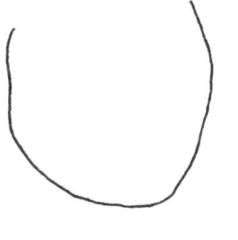

COAT HANGER OR PIANO WIRE

STRING SMALL FISH THROUGH
MOUTH AND GILL

CORD TIED TO WIRE

WEIGHT

BEND OVER ENDS OF WIRE
FORMING A CIRCLE

ALLOW WIRE (WITH FISH) TO GO
TO BOTTOM

FIGURE 3   **LIVE FISH RING**

CHAPTER 4

CRAB TRAPS AND CRAB POTS

There are various and different types of crab traps and crab pots used when crabbing. These traps and pots produce from good to excellent results but the personal challenge of the contest, that of pitting the sportsman's abilities, and mental powers against the crab's natural and wiley instincts, is completely lacking. Most commercial crabbers today use these crab pots or traps solely in taking crabs. It is a business with them and not a sport.

The words "trap" and "pot" are commonly considered synonymous and interchangeable. Webster's Dictionary defines the words as follows:

Trap: "A device for taking game or other animals, to catch, to entrap"

Pot: "An enclosed framework of wire, wood or wicker, for catching fish, crabs and lobsters"

A very fine distinction in interpretation does exist, however, whereby a trap **may** or **may not** be a pot. If you wish to understand the distinction between the two, ask yourself the following question: Can the crab enter and leave this piece of equipment at any time prior to a physical act by the crabber? If the answer is "yes," then the gear being used is called a trap. If the answer is "no," it is termed and referred to as a pot.

Figures 1 and 2 show two kinds of wire traps. You will note that when traps are on the bottom, all four side panels are open and the crabs may enter and leave at will since there is nothing to hold them inside at this time. However, when the crabber pulls on the cord or rope, the side panels are pulled up and they close tightly against the frame. If, at this moment, the crabs are eating the bait, they will be trapped inside and cannot get out unless the panels are opened again.

In Figure 3 there is only one large opening through which the crabs may enter and leave at will. If the crabber pulls upward rapidly, the front (open) end rises first. The crabs inside, if any, will then try to fight the upward motion and go to the closed bottom of the trap in an effort to escape.

The Maryland crab pot is an enclosed framework of wire with four openings as shown in Figure 4. These openings are so constructed that when the crabs enter to eat the bait, they cannot escape. They instead become immediately trapped therein. When the crabs find they cannot leave the same way they entered, they float upward and go through the openings of the inner wire portion. They have then become permanently trapped in the upper portion of the pot.

Another type of crab pot is shown in Figure 5. This type of pot differs in design from the Maryland crab pot and is used mostly on the West Coast to catch Dungeness crabs. The theory is similar. When the crabs enter either of the two funnel-type openings in search of bait, they are unable to exit through these funnel openings and become "prisoners" of the pot.

The employment of a crab trap is simple and requires little physical exertion. It weighs only a few pounds when baited. First, be sure the cords connecting the panels (sides) to the main cord operate and close properly. Be certain too that there is enough cord to allow the trap to go to the bottom depth and enough extra cord to fall loose on bottom and to secure the line on top. This is the same procedure you would follow when using hand lines (see Chapter 2). The bait should be tied tightly inside the trap with string or wire and the trap dropped into the water, where it will soon rest on the bottom. The cord or rope should be long enough so that the end on the top side can be secured. When the trap rests on the bottom and the cord is loose enough, the side panels will open (fall down) and also lie flat on the bottom. This allows the crabs easy ingress and egress to the bait (see Figures 1 and 2). After waiting about five or ten minutes, pull the trap quickly upward to the surface, holding the line tightly hand over hand. This action pulls up the cords holding the side panels and presses them firmly against the framework of the trap. Any crabs that are inside the trap at this time will be unable to escape. The cord must be held tightly when the trap is being pulled out of the water to prevent the side panels from opening. The trap, once it is removed from the water, may be taken to your basket or receptacle. Open one panel with one hand and allow the crabs to fall or drop into the basket. Some shaking may be necessary. All illegal crabs must be removed from the receptacle and returned to the water. They may be removed by hand, gloved hands or tongs. If you catch a "softie" or soft-shell (blue claw), separate it from the hard-shell crabs and keep in a separate container. When this has been accomplished, check your bait, replace if necessary, and then throw or drop your trap back into the water and wait again. Continue this procedure until you have a "basket full of crabs" or decide to quit crabbing for the day.

The advantage of using a trap over a hand line is that a trap can be used in all kinds of weather such as rain and wind, choppy, rough or murky water conditions, or any other unfavorable conditions that might prevail. The crabs are trapped immediately when the panels are closed as you have observed in Figures 1 and 2. This action occurs below the surface. Unlike the possible occurrences experienced when using the hand line method of crabbing, the crabs cannot drop off, get scared or be intimidated by the weather conditions above or on the surface (see Part II, Chapter 2).

HOW TO USE A CRAB POT

The crab pot is a much larger and heavier piece of equipment used to catch crabs than a trap. The Maryland crab pot is cubicle, generally 2'x2'x2' and, when baited and weighted, might weigh fifteen pounds or more. It takes more physical exertion than does a crab trap to operate, but, unlike the trap, it is only brought to the surface once or twice a day. Sometimes it is left on the bottom for as long as twelve to twenty-four hours or more. The end of the nylon rope is attached to a marked floating buoy so the location can be found and the pot retrieved. When the pot is pulled from the water and it contains many crabs, it may weigh thirty, forty or fifty pounds. Those persons who are not sturdily built may require assistance when pulling up a crab pot.

The Maryland crab pot is baited from the bottom with several oily fish (Menhaden) as shown in Figure 6. This is done by turning the pot on its side, stuffing the bait into the wire container (inside the pot — see Figure 6-A), and closing the opening by securing the flap (see Figure 6-B) under the rubber tubing (see Figure 6-C). The pot must then be turned over, making sure that the rope (see Figure 6-E) is long enough and that the buoy is tied firmly to the end and marked properly according to state laws or with your name, color or number. The pot is then dropped into the water. When you return to your buoy or marker, pull the pot up and into your boat. It is only necessary to push down on the top when opening the pot. This disengages the wire hook (see Figure 6-A). While holding top to one side of the pot (see Figure 7), pull up on top. This allows an opening along one side. Then turn the pot over and shake crabs into the basket. Again, cull and check all crabs for "keepers" and return all others to the water. Rebait the bait container and close (also close hook on top of the pot) and return the pot to the water for the next catch.

A similar procedure is used with the crab pot in Figure 5 with one exception: the bait is put into the bait box from the top and the half-hinged top is secured with a wire hook. The pot is then dropped into the water, making certain that a marked buoy is on the other end of the rope.

Crab pots should be attended, pulled (retrieved) and checked every day or at most, within a few days, depending upon the weather. Keep in mind the crabs are trapped inside and will not live too long without food. Remember too that they are cannibalistic and will begin to kill and eat each other, thereby reducing the amount of your catch.

When using either of these methods of crabbing, make sure you are familiar with the state laws. You may or may not be able to crab with pots or traps without a license, the number of each to be used may be limited, and the requirements for marking buoys may be different.

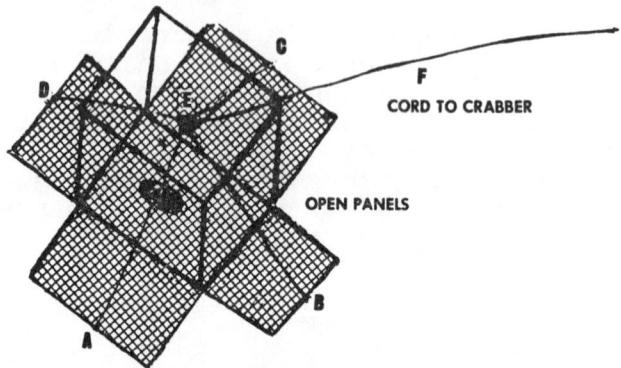

ALL PANEL CORDS TIED TO E

C

F

CORD TO CRABBER

D

E

OPEN PANELS

B

A

This is how the square type wire trap looks when on the bottom. All panels (A, B, C and D) are open and flat on bottom. This allows crabs to enter, eat and leave. They can come and go as they please, as they are not entrapped in this position.

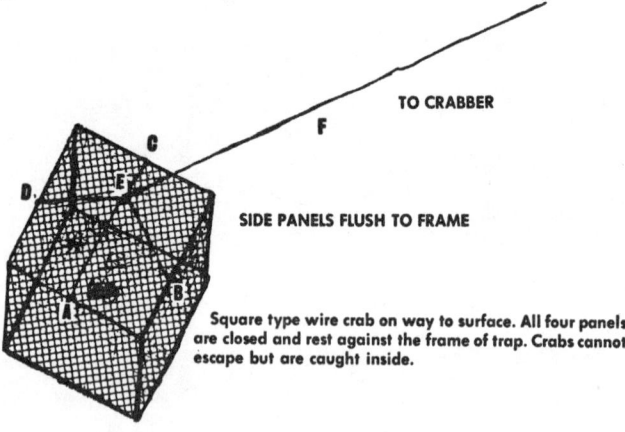

TO CRABBER

F

C

E

SIDE PANELS FLUSH TO FRAME

D

A

B

Square type wire crab on way to surface. All four panels are closed and rest against the frame of trap. Crabs cannot escape but are caught inside.

FIGURE 1   **SQUARE TYPE WIRE TRAP**

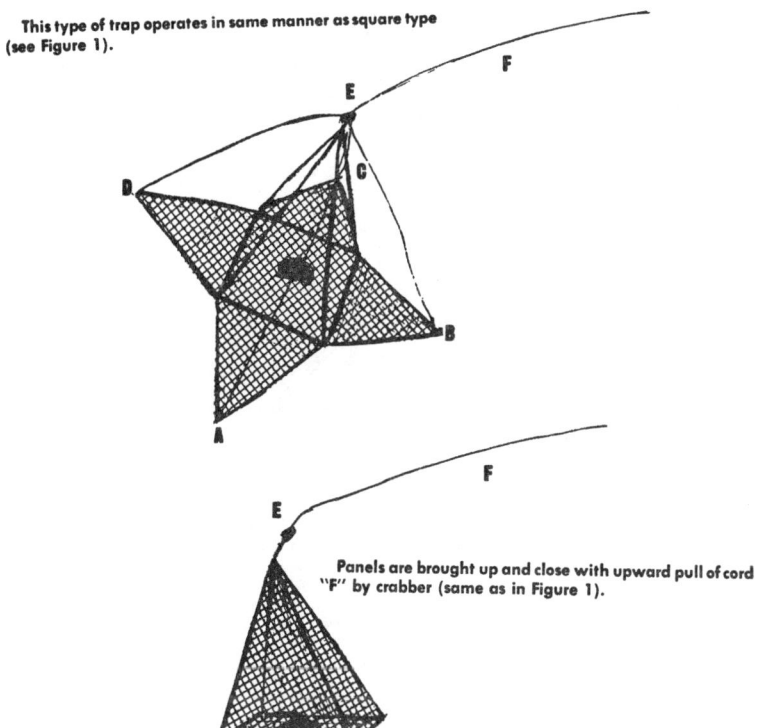

This type of trap operates in same manner as square type (see Figure 1).

Panels are brought up and close with upward pull of cord "F" by crabber (same as in Figure 1).

FIGURE 2 **PYRAMID TYPE WIRE TRAP**

79

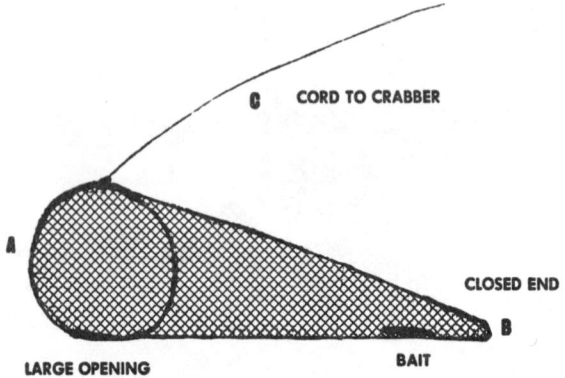

CORD TO CRABBER

C

A

CLOSED END

B

LARGE OPENING

BAIT

In this type of trap there is only one large open end. The crabs can leave by this opening at any time. The rest of the basket trap is completely enclosed. When Line "C" is pulled rapidly upward, the open end, "A", goes up first as the cord is tied to top of opening. The crabs try to escape the upward movement but tend to go to the bottom of Trap "B", where they cannot escape and are trapped.

FIGURE 3   **OPEN END WIRE BASKET**

80

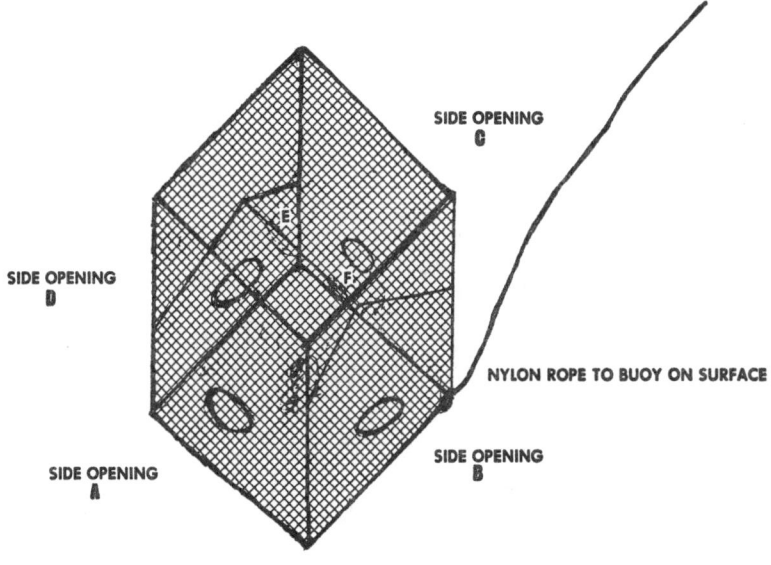

SIDE OPENING
C

SIDE OPENING
D

SIDE OPENING
A

SIDE OPENING
B

NYLON ROPE TO BUOY ON SURFACE

This crab pot has four specially constructed side openings
(A, B, C and D) for the crabs to enter. They do not exit
through these openings, but float up through openings "E"
and "F" in the inside wire to the upper part of pot and are
trapped in this area of the pot.

FIGURE 4

MARYLAND CRAB POT

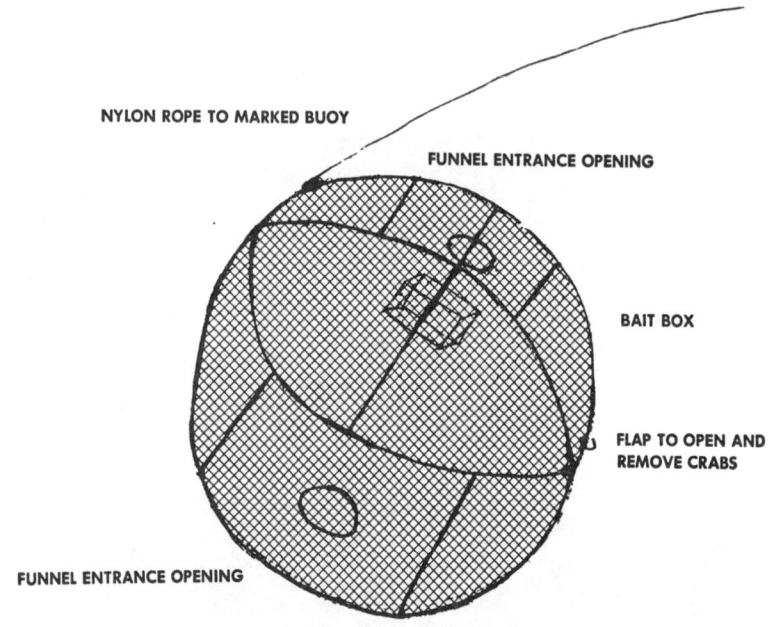

NYLON ROPE TO MARKED BUOY

FUNNEL ENTRANCE OPENING

BAIT BOX

FLAP TO OPEN AND
REMOVE CRABS

FUNNEL ENTRANCE OPENING

This type pot, used on the West Coast, operates similarly
to the Maryland crab pots, but it varies in construction and
does not have an inner holding area as does the Maryland
crab pot.

FIGURE 5   **ROUND WIRE POT**

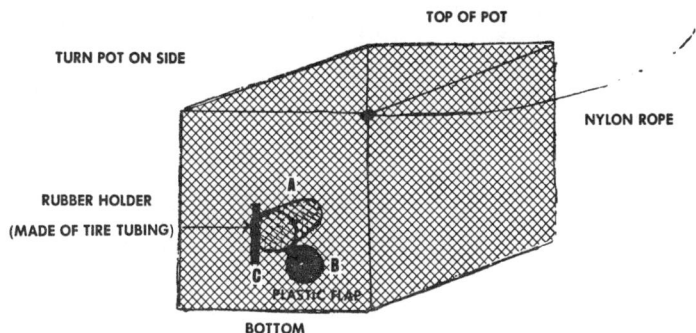

TOP OF POT

TURN POT ON SIDE

NYLON ROPE

RUBBER HOLDER
(MADE OF TIRE TUBING)

A

C B
PLASTIC FLAP

BOTTOM

Insert bait into wire bait container "A". Close Flap "B" by
placing under rubber tubing "C", turn pot right side up and
drop into water.

FIGURE 6   **HOW TO BAIT POT**

83

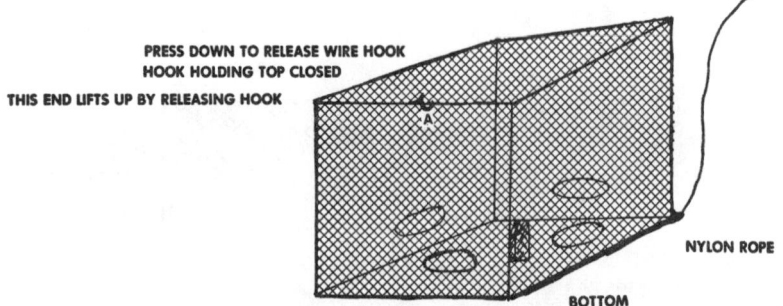

PRESS DOWN TO RELEASE WIRE HOOK
HOOK HOLDING TOP CLOSED

THIS END LIFTS UP BY RELEASING HOOK

A

NYLON ROPE

BOTTOM

TO REMOVE CRABS: Press down on top portion of pot,
release Hook "A" and pull up.

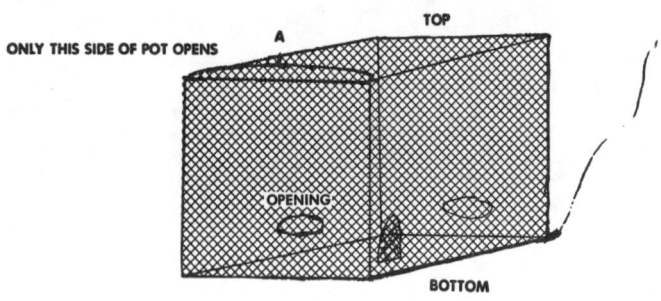

ONLY THIS SIDE OF POT OPENS

A

TOP

OPENING

BOTTOM

FIGURE 7   **MARYLAND CRAB POT**

84

CHAPTER 5

TROTLINES

Hand dip trotlines were used exclusively by commercial crabbers from 1870 to 1929, but this method has since been almost entirely replaced by crab pots and crab traps. Only a few sportsmen use the former method today, but it is an interesting, enjoyable, productive way to catch crabs.

A hand trotline is a baited, hookless, long line that is usually anchored on the bottom and attached to anchored floats (buoys) at either end. They may also be anchored to some permanent objects such as trees, docks, or stakes driven into the sand or mud bottom (see Figure 1,A,B and C). The length of the line varies with the user but may be from one hundred feet to a mile long, depending upon the area and location. Generally the sportsman uses a line one hundred to three hundred feet in length. The line (rope) can be cotton, sisal, hemp or nylon, with a diameter of one-eighth to three-sixteenth of an inch. This long line (trotline) can be baited in two ways: (1) by tying bait directly to the line or slipping bait into strands of the cotton or hemp rope; (2) by tying the bait to the ends of six to twenty-four inch lateral lines fastened to the main line called "snoods" (see Figure 2-A and B). The best bait to use is fresh beef tripe (stomach), eels or trash fish, but salted tripe, hog jowls, eels and pig ears are productive, last longer and work almost as well (see Part II, Chapter 3).

Crabs may be caught with a trotline in shallow water, moderately deep water or deep water. The crabber can be standing in the water (depending upon the depth), or he may operate from a boat. Crabs will not usually be found in the shallow waters in extremely hot weather but will retreat to the deeper cooler waters. For this reason, it is important to know your weather conditions. The use of a trotline is similar to an individual hand line (see Part II, Chapter 2).

When using trotlines from a boat, the lines must be placed and established in the water as shown in Figure 1-A and B. The trotlines usually are set parallel to the shore and fished with the tide, up or down river. If fished during slack tides, they can be fished in any direction, usually perpendicular to shore (see

85

Figure 1-B). The crabber must first approach the buoy (see Figure 3-A). He must then pick up the trotline with a short-handled hook, take the line in hand and then, hand over hand, pull in the line. As the boat moves along the line, the baits are raised to the surface and crabs clinging to the baits are scooped up by a scoop or dip net. One person can perform this feat, but the scoop net must always remain in one hand and ready to snare its prey. Normally, it is much better for two crabbers to work together so that one may pull the line and the other can stand by with the scoop or dip net. A small mesh wire net is best for this operation as the crabs cannot cling to the wire as they do to cotton or nylon netting. The scooping crabber must be quick because the crabs will drop off the baits immediately when the baits break the surface of the water. He must scoop the crab, deposit him in the basket and be ready for the next one in a hurry. The trotline is allowed to drop back into the water as the boat moves toward the other float. When the whole line is fished (crabbed), the crabber then waits a while (depending on the length of line) and then returns to Buoy "A" to begin the next run along the trotline. Baits should always be checked at the end of a day's crabbing and renewed or replaced if they are to be used the next day. The line is then coiled into a tub or barrel and sprinkled well with salt to protect the bait and line from rotting.

When using a trotline in shallow water without a boat, the crabber first sets his line between two stakes or two permanent objects (see Figure 1-C). Then he "walks the line" with scoop net and a floating basket tied to his waist (see Figure 4)." Hand over hand, he pulls the baits to the surface, scoops the crabs and deposits them quickly into the floating basket. This method is more of a chore and taxes one's endurance and coordination to the utmost—but it certainly is fun! It is much easier to work this line with two persons also and for the same reasons set forth in the preceding paragraph.

All illegal crabs should be returned to the water and the crabber should know if trotlines are permissable to use without obtaining a license.

A patent-dip trotline differs from a hand-dip trotline only in the method used to dip crabs out of the water. The patent-dip is a large net attached to a boom on a boat which may be hoisted or lowered to the surface of the water. The use of this type of equipment requires no individual hand-scooping and is used strictly by commercial crabbers and is shown only for information and not for discussion (see Figure 5).

Why not try a trotline the next time you go crabbing? It's fun and it's different.

A   USE OF BOAT

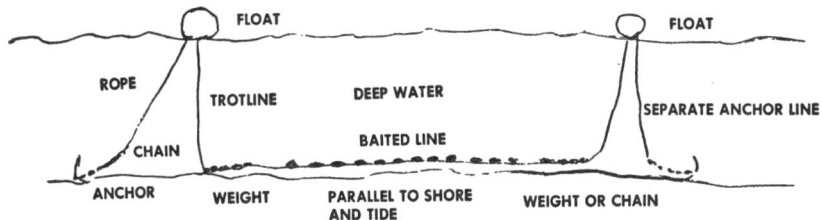

FLOAT

FLOAT

ROPE

TROTLINE

DEEP WATER

SEPARATE ANCHOR LINE

CHAIN

BAITED LINE

ANCHOR

WEIGHT

PARALLEL TO SHORE
AND TIDE

WEIGHT OR CHAIN

B   USE OF BOAT

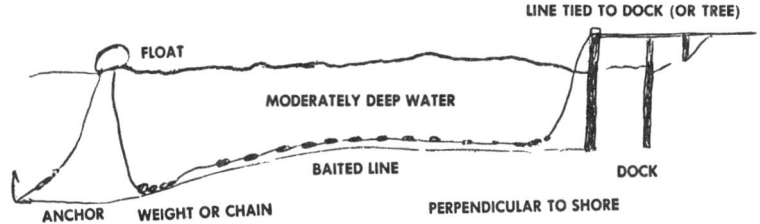

LINE TIED TO DOCK (OR TREE)

FLOAT

MODERATELY DEEP WATER

BAITED LINE

DOCK

ANCHOR

WEIGHT OR CHAIN

PERPENDICULAR TO SHORE

C   BY STANDING IN THE WATER

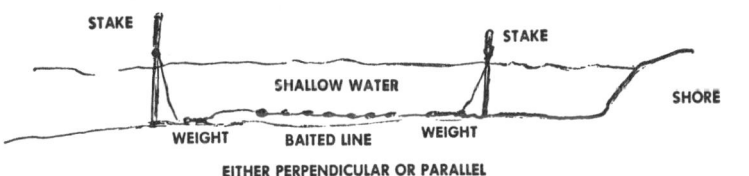

STAKE

STAKE

SHALLOW WATER

SHORE

WEIGHT

BAITED LINE

WEIGHT

EITHER PERPENDICULAR OR PARALLEL

FIGURE 1   **TROT LINES**

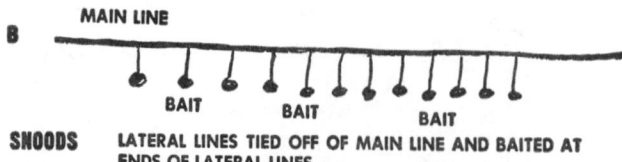

BAIT   BAIT

A

BAIT TIED DIRECTLY TO LINE 2 TO 6 FEET APART

MAIN LINE

B

BAIT   BAIT   BAIT

SNOODS   LATERAL LINES TIED OFF OF MAIN LINE AND BAITED AT
           ENDS OF LATERAL LINES

BAITS AND LINES 2 TO 6 FEET APART

FIGURE 2   **TROT LINES**

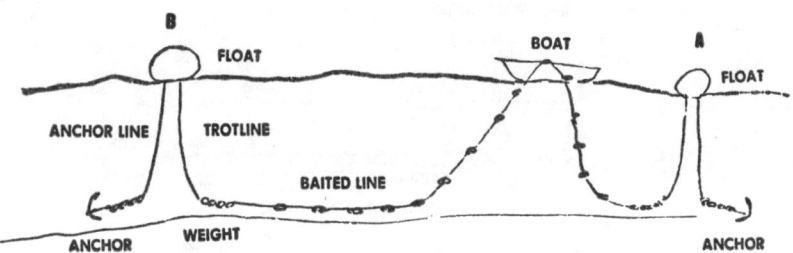

Main line with bait is pulled to surface and crabs are
scooped into net and dumped into basket. Line is
continuously pulled along entire length. After scooping
crabs line is allowed to drop back into the water.

After line is fished crabber returns to Float A and starts his
operation over again.

FIGURE 3   **TROTLINE BETWEEN TWO BUOYS**

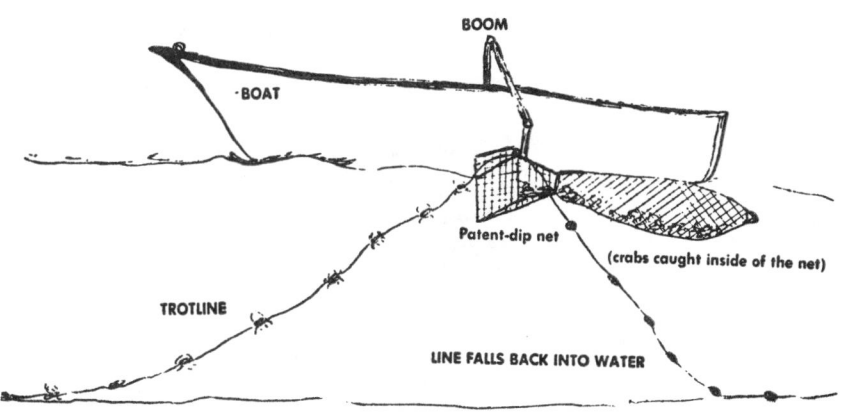

BOOM

·BOAT

Patent-dip net

(crabs caught inside of the net)

TROTLINE

LINE FALLS BACK INTO WATER

No individual netting is necessary with this equipment

FIGURE 4   **PATENT-DIP TROT LINE**

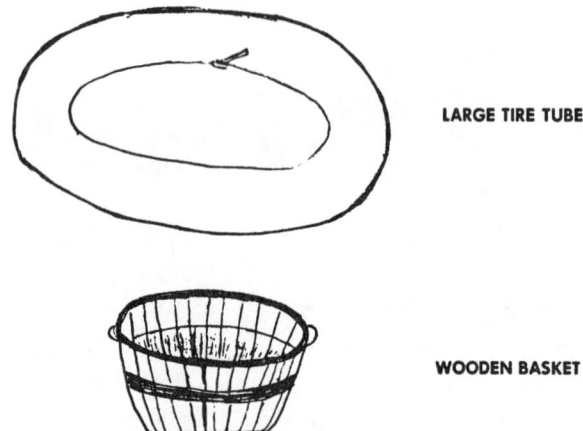

LARGE TIRE TUBE

WOODEN BASKET

Place basket tightly inside of tire tube.

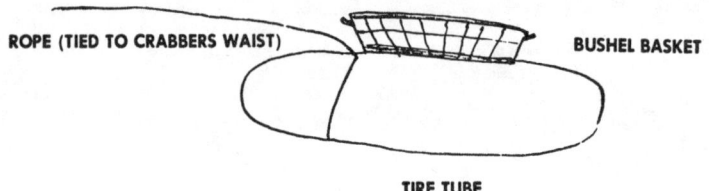

ROPE (TIED TO CRABBERS WAIST)

BUSHEL BASKET

TIRE TUBE

Rope is tied to crabbers waist and is pulled on surface of water.

FIGURE 5   **FLOATING BASKET**

CHAPTER 6

SEINES

A seine is a large net used in catching fish and crabs. Seines come in all sizes, shapes and forms. The most often used by crabbers is a rectangular seine four feet wide by twenty-four feet long with mesh openings of one-eighth of an inch to an inch in diameter (see Figure 1-A). Small floats are tied to this seine along the top at three foot intervals. This keeps the top of the seine floating on top of the water. One-half ounce lead weights (tube type) are added to the bottom of the seine and are pressed on at one-foot intervals. These weights hold the bottom of the seine to the water bottom (see Figure 1-B). A five to six foot pole is then securely tied to each side of the seine. The bottom part of the pole protrudes about two inches below the bottom end of the seine; the remaining length extends above the floats (see Figure 1-C).

The seine described above is fairly simple to handle but its utilization requires two people, one on each pole. Seining is performed IN THE WATER, so appropriate attire should be worn. From my own past experience, "sneakers" (tennis shoes) are strongly recommended. They not only protect the seiner's feet from sharp shells, broken glass or other underwater objects, but they provide protection from the hungry crabs as well who may mistake a bare toe for an attractive piece of raw bait.

Now to go seining! First, stretch out the seine (with the poles length-wise and full length) flat on the ground or beach with floats nearest the water line (see Figure 2-A). Next, each person takes a pole in both hands and lifts it up so that the seine is parallel to the ground (see Figure 2-B). Both persons then move into the water together, holding their position (seine between them and at full length with seine and poles parallel to and above the surface of the water as shown in Figure 2-B)

When the water is almost chest-deep, both persons release the bottom ends of the poles, and the bottom of the seine (end with weights) descends to the ocean or water floor. Each person faces the shore and, with one hand about two feet from the bottom of the pole and the other near the top of the seine (floats), allow the top part of the pole to go backwards until it is at a 60° angle to the bottom. The top part angles backwards and the bottom part angles forward (see Figure 3-A). Both persons then move simultaneously toward the shore dragging the bottom part of the pole through the sand or mud by applying more pressure on the hand that is two feet from the seine's bottom. As both move inshore at the same time, they move slightly toward each other. The seine will flare or billow out in the rear forming a large pocket (see Figure 3-B). When both reach the shoreline, they should be approximately fourteen to eighteen feet apart. The seine is then dragged up on the beach, letting the top part of the poles fall forward and inward toward the center of the seine (see Figure 4-A.) This allows the net to drop over the crabs so they cannot escape. The crabs should be removed one by one from the netting, inside or under, and placed in a basket. Hand removal of crabs is a barrel of fun and crabbers may find themselves chasing a few of their catch, as some of these fast-moving, perceptive creatures may find their way out of the seine and scamper back toward the water (see Part II, Chapter 1). All illegal crabs must be returned to the water. When all crabs have been removed from the seine, the poles should be grasped again with both hands, stretched to full length and shaken out. Then you are ready to follow the same procedure for the next dragging, seining operation, working your way up and down the shoreline area in sections.

This method of catching crabs does require physical exertion as you can see, but it certainly is an excellent form of exercise. If it becomes fatiguing after a time, rest between catches, take an invigorating swim or just sun-bathe and enjoy the great outdoors!

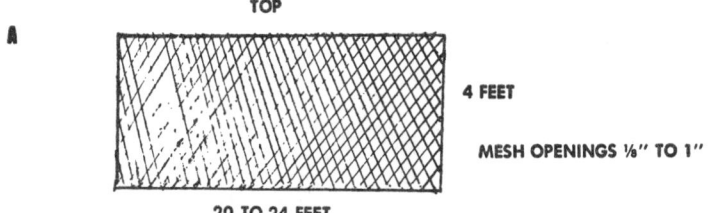

TOP

A

4 FEET

MESH OPENINGS ⅛" TO 1"

20 TO 24 FEET

Rectangular seine 4X24 feet with mesh openings of ⅛" to 1 inch in width.

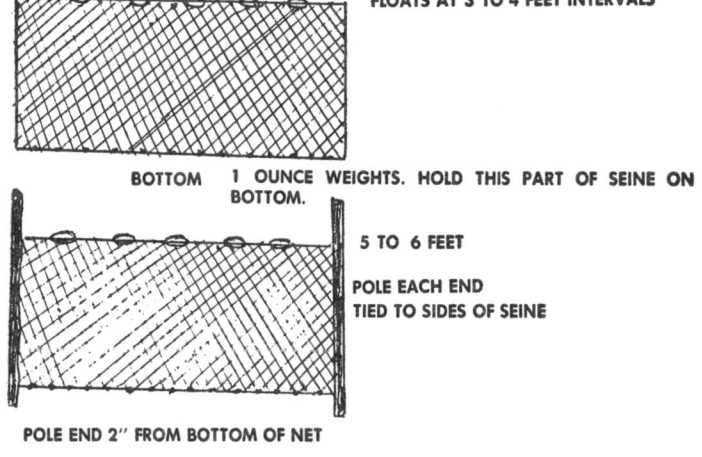

FLOATS AT 3 TO 4 FEET INTERVALS

BOTTOM 1 OUNCE WEIGHTS. HOLD THIS PART OF SEINE ON BOTTOM.

5 TO 6 FEET

POLE EACH END TIED TO SIDES OF SEINE

POLE END 2" FROM BOTTOM OF NET

FIGURE 1   SEINES

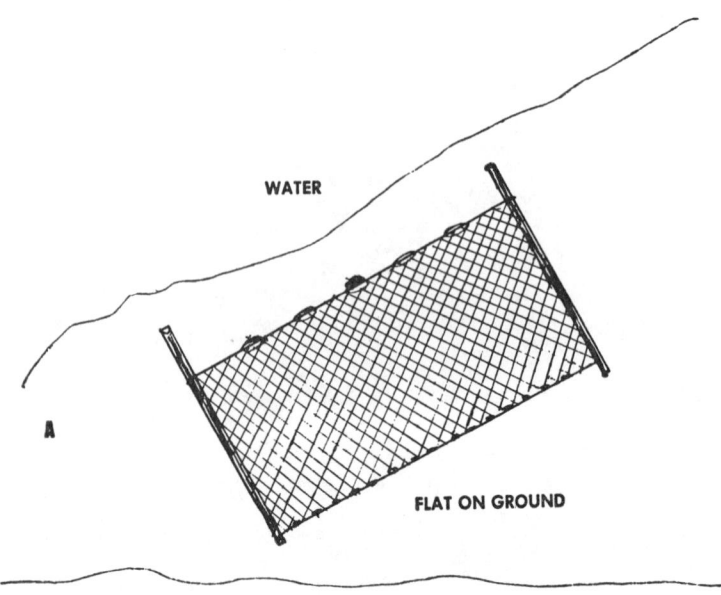

WATER

A

FLAT ON GROUND

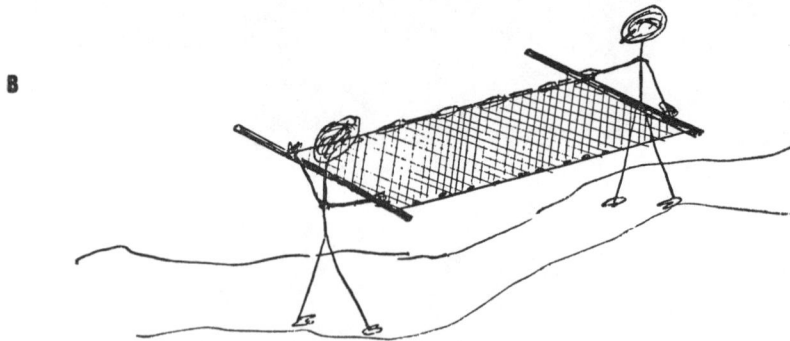

B

Walk into water with poles and seine parallel to water
Go out to a depth not quite chest high.

FIGURE 2   **SEINES**

94

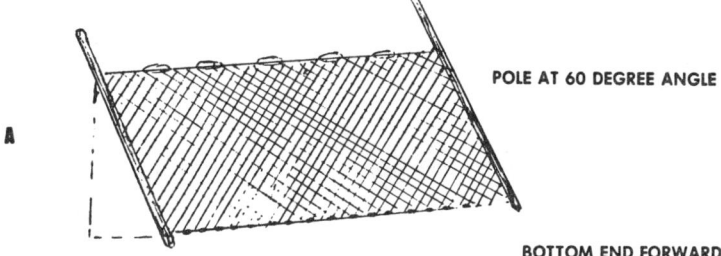

A

POLE AT 60 DEGREE ANGLE

BOTTOM END FORWARD

Person on each end face to shore with net between

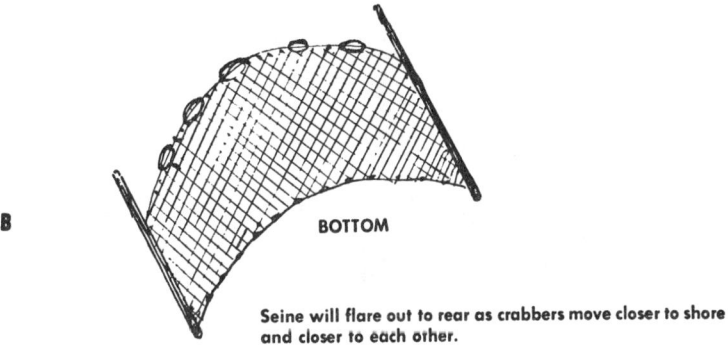

B

BOTTOM

Seine will flare out to rear as crabbers move closer to shore and closer to each other.

By the time both reach shore they should still be parallel to each other and 14 to 18 feet apart.

FIGURE 3   **SEINES**

95

A

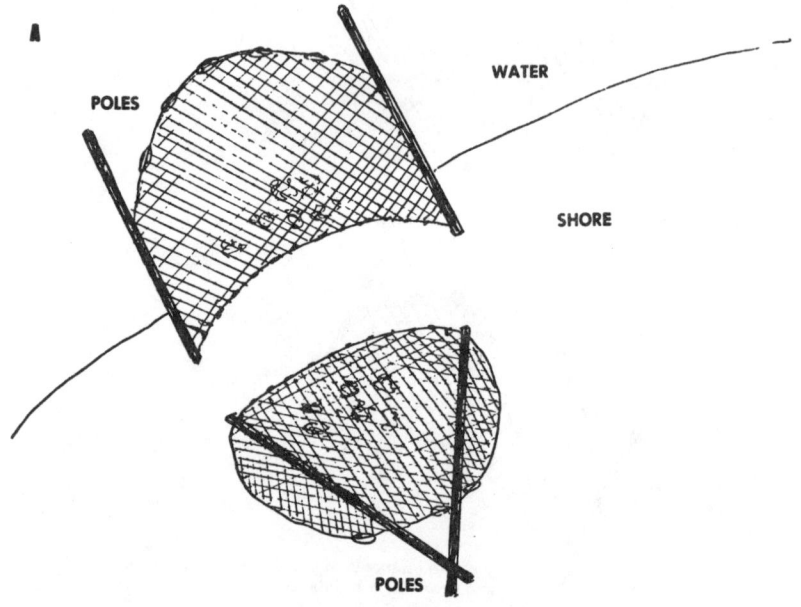

POLES

WATER

SHORE

POLES

Allow poles to fall forward and toward each other so that
crabs are entangled and caught in the netting.

FIGURE 4   **SEINES**

CHAPTER 7

CRAB RINGS

A crab ring is actually a folding, collapsible, weighted net-enclosed basket used to catch crabs. In reality, it is another form and design of a crab trap. Crab rings are very popular and are used extensively on the West Coast to catch Dungeness crabs. Crab rings have been introduced to the East Coast in recent years that are smaller in size than west coast models, but they are still not as popular with east coast crabbers as the conventional wire traps described in Part II, Chapter 4.

The use of a crab ring is simple and easy and requires a minimum of effort on the part of the crabber.

The crab ring comes in a variety of sizes but the basic construction is similar. It consists of two circular metal hoops, one smaller than the other (see Figure 1-A). The area within the circumference of the bottom (smaller) ring is enclosed with heavy chicken wire (see Figure 1-B). Both rings are attached together with cotton or nylon netting of various mesh openings as shown in Figure 1-C. Nylon ropes are attached to the top ring at A, B and C, joined at Point D and tied (see Figure 2-A). A rope long enough to reach the bottom and to be held or secured above the surface is then tied to D (see Figure 2-B). The bait is tied to the chicken wire of the bottom ring as illustrated in Figure 3. The ring lies flat on the bottom when it is thrown into the water (see Figure 3-B). The crabs then enter to eat the bait. When the ring is pulled upward, the top ring moves up first, forming a basket effect. The crabs are hopelessly trapped inside the netting between the top and bottom rings (see Figure 4).

This is all there is to crabbing with a crab ring. Again, just bait the ring, throw it into the water and after waiting a few minutes, pull the rope to the surface rapidly. Deposit the crabs that have been caught into a basket, check the bait, return illegal crabs to the water, throw the ring back into the water and wait! This is a lazy, but often productive, way to catch crabs; anyone can do it.

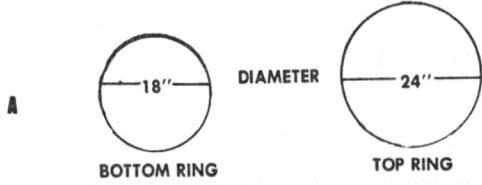

A

DIAMETER

BOTTOM RING

TOP RING

Bottom and top rings are of ¾" solid metal

Electrical (rubber) **tape** is wrapped around entire circumference of each ring.

B

CHICKEN WIRE

Rings act as weights to hold entire crab ring to bottom.

Heavy chicken wire covers inside area and is wired to the bottom ring

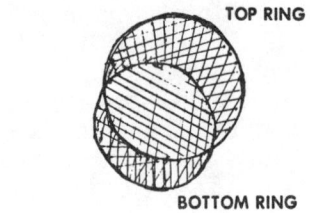

C

TOP RING

BOTTOM RING

NETTING CONNECTS TOP RING TO BOTTOM RING

Larger Crab rings measure 30" Bottom - 36" top ring.

FIGURE 1   **CRAB RINGS**

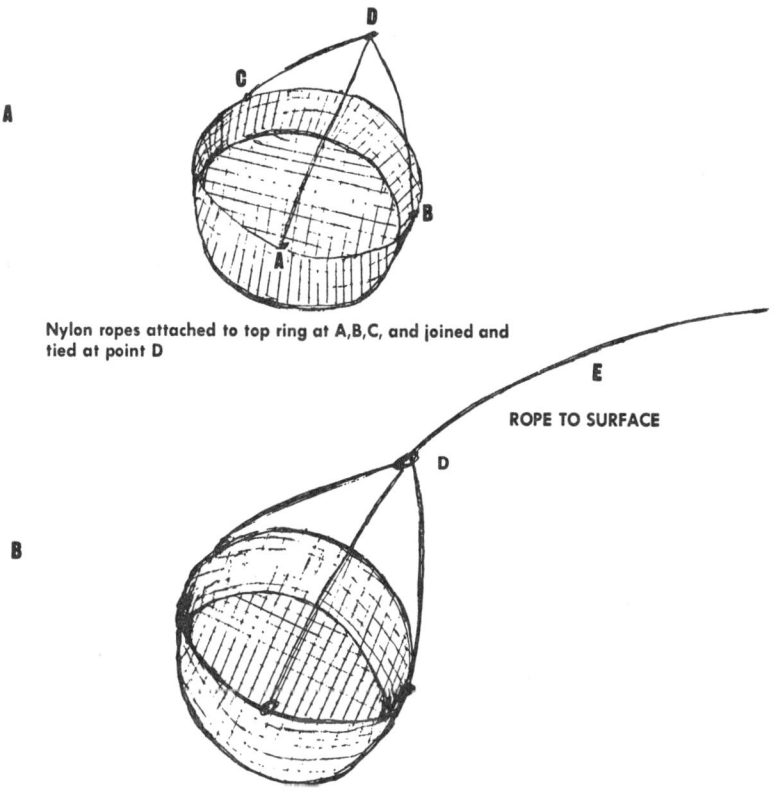

A

Nylon ropes attached to top ring at A,B,C, and joined and
tied at point D

B

ROPE TO SURFACE

Bait tied to chicken wire on bottom ring.

FIGURE 2   **CRAB RINGS**

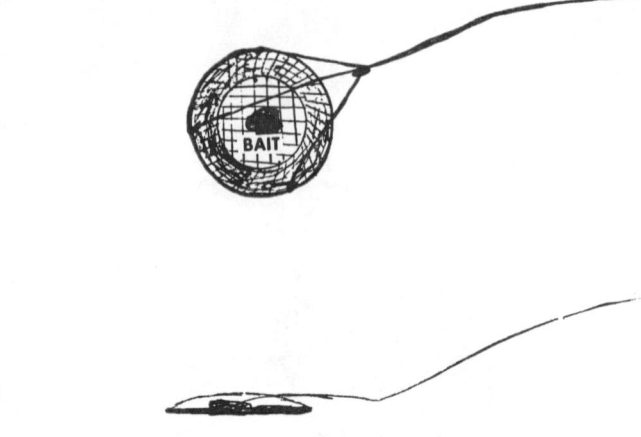

A

B

CRAB RING ON BOTTOM

Both rings netting and rope lie flat on bottom

FIGURE 3   **CRAB RINGS**

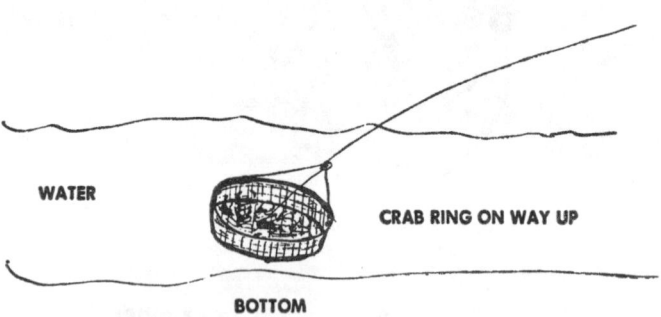

WATER

CRAB RING ON WAY UP

BOTTOM

When rope is pulled up rapidly top ring is elevated first (with pull of rope) and forms a basket effect to entrap the crabs within.

FIGURE 4   **CRAB RING**

CHAPTER 8

SCOOP OR DIP NETS

Scoop and dip nets are one and the same. (**Dip:** to drive or plunge into liquid; **Scoop:** to lift up with something hollow).

A scoop or dip net comes in various handle lengths, circumference sizes and hollow depths (see Figure 1). The netting may be of cotton, nylon, plastic screening or small mesh wire.

The use of the scoop or dip net was described in Part II, Chapter 2 in connection with hand lines and again in Chapter 5 when discussing trotlines. A scoop or dip net can also be used by itself to catch crabs. No line or bait is required. This method can be done during the daylight hours in a number of ways:

(1) Chasing or running after the crabs in the water

This method is by far the most exciting and does offer a continuing challenge to your scooping talents and proficiency, as well as your athletic capabilities and prowess. The offshore waters must be shallow (between twelve and fourteen inches deep), very clear with no surface activity (wind), and the bottom must be very solid if you are crabbing with only a scoop net. You must be able to see the crabs moving along the sandy bottom in order to chase them. With scoop net in hand, look downward as you walk through the shallow water parallel to the shore. When you see a crab (he probably will see you first and start retreating from you), pursue him and be ready to scoop him into your net when you are close enough to make contact. Crabs can move extremely fast along the bottom, so be ready for a "chase". When the crab is within range of your scoop net, scoop the net down into the water and into the top layer of sand, use your fast-turning wrist action and bring the net up and out of the water. Should you fail to catch your crab, this plucky, "fighting" little animal may very well decide to become the "attacker". You may be in for a big surprise if you do not have protective sneakers on your feet. A quick bite on a toe and the chase will be reversed immediately! Onlookers will be treated to a hilarious and entertaining exhibition of a crab chasing, howling man! When you do catch a crab, place him in your basket on shore, return him to the water if he is not a legal catch, and search some more for these active, fast-moving bottom inhabitants.

(2) Scooping from a boat

A long-handled scoop net is used when scooping from a boat. As you travel slowly on the surface of the water, usually in and among the shallow and high grass or reed-protected marshes, you will see crabs resting or moving slowly on top of the water, in, along and among these high grass marshes. The object at this moment is to get your boat in as closely as possible (a flat-bottom boat is best), and scoop the crab from the top or from the grasses with the extra length of your long-handled net. You will find that a great majority of the crabs caught in these areas will be "soft-shell" or "busters" that have moved to these locations to shed and gain cover and for protection from other crabs and fish.

(3) From shore, along bulkheads, docks piers and seawalls

While walking along the latter four constructions mentioned above, crabs may be seen clinging to the pilings or outcroppings. Be certain you can reach them with your net, then scoop down, alongside, under and up. This method sometimes is difficult as the obstructions (walls, pilings, etc.) may interfere with the smooth and complete follow-through motion of the net.

Scooping takes practice, so go out and have a "scooping" and a "whooping" good time!

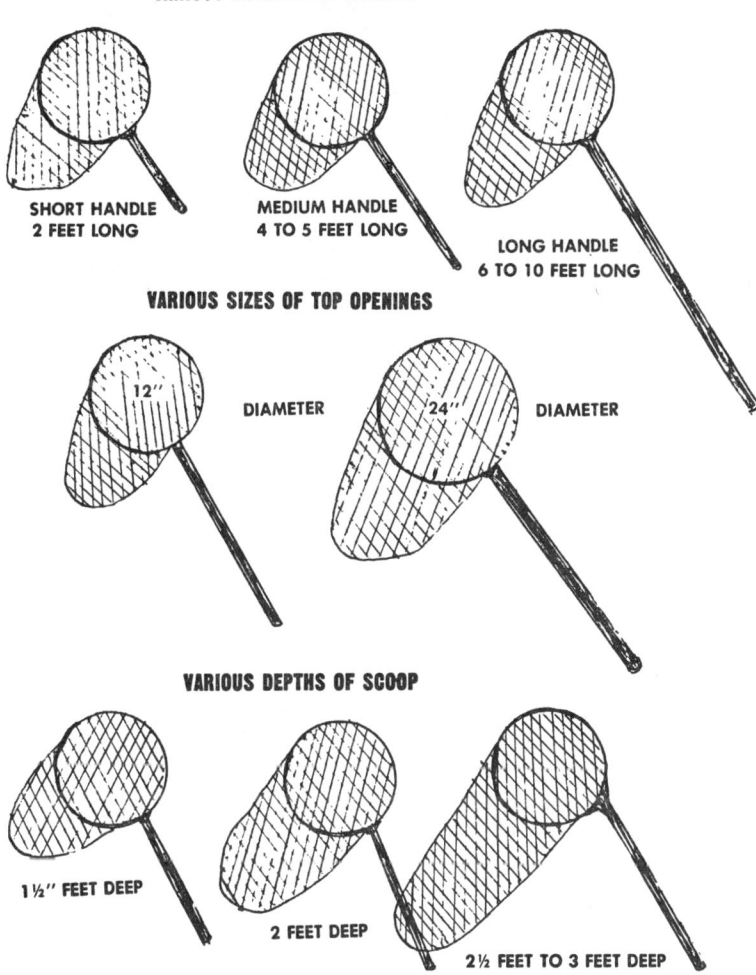

VARIOUS LENGTHS OF HANDLES

SHORT HANDLE
2 FEET LONG

MEDIUM HANDLE
4 TO 5 FEET LONG

LONG HANDLE
6 TO 10 FEET LONG

VARIOUS SIZES OF TOP OPENINGS

12" DIAMETER

24" DIAMETER

VARIOUS DEPTHS OF SCOOP

1½" FEET DEEP

2 FEET DEEP

2½ FEET TO 3 FEET DEEP

FIGURE 1

SCOOP OR DIP NETS

103

CHAPTER 9

NIGHT CRABBING (WITH ILLUMINATION)

Although crabbing is commonly a "sun-up to sun-down" sport, it may be enjoyed during the evening hours as well with the help of artificial illumination and a scoop net. This should be good news to would- be crabbers who, because of their employment or other daytime commitments, can only participate in certain nocturnal sport activities. Night crabbing can be very rewarding and offers a relaxing change of pace from mundane routines. A very bright dry cell flashlight or other battery- operated light and the scoop net described in Chapter 8 are all you will need. It is always good to have an extra supply of batteries along too. The stronger and brighter the light, the more effective it will be. Remember, you have to see the crabs before you can net them and you must always be certain the scoop net is long enough to reach into the water. A long-hand-led scoop net ranging from six to ten feet is preferable.

Crabbing at night can be performed from any of the locations mentioned in previous chapters (from a pier, dock, bulkhead, while standing in the water, or from a boat on the surface of the water). It is possible for one person to handle both the light and the scoop, but some find it more enjoyable and much easier when two or more join in the sport.

Crabbing at night with a light is achieved in the following manner: First, select your location. Then turn on the light and focus it on a spot on the surface of the water about one to twelve feet from your position. The water should be quite shallow and calm (one to ten feet deep) and the beam of light strong enough to reach the bottom or near-bottom of the water. Crabs on the bottom and in the vicinity of the light are attracted to its beam as it enters and penetrates the water and they will follow it to or near the water surface. If the crab is out of reach of your scoop net, you can coax him in closer by keeping the beam in front of him and slowly moving it inward and closer to your location. When the crab is within reach of your net, scoop down, alongside, under and up, remembering to use your fast wrist action. Each location or area can be worked for long periods of time. When crabbing slacks off, move to another location and try your luck again, operating your light in the same manner and covering all surface as shown in Figure 1.

Mosquitoes or bugs may join you in your night-time crabbing activities (the light and your sweet blood will attract them also), so be forewarned and be prepared. Carry a bottle of an effective insect repellent with you. You will be very glad you did!

Night crabbing is different and will be a true test of your talents. The object, however, is to have fun and to enjoy nature clothed in another of its many costumes. Perhaps you may wish to combine a beach or boat party on the bay with crabbing. Add some "nibbles", lots of cold liquid refreshments, good fellowship and you have all the ingredients for a memorable evening. Just think! What could be more delightful on a lovely balmy, moonlit summer night than good friends breaking into melodious voice and singing, "By the Light of the Silvery Moon"? The crabs will offer no objections whatever!

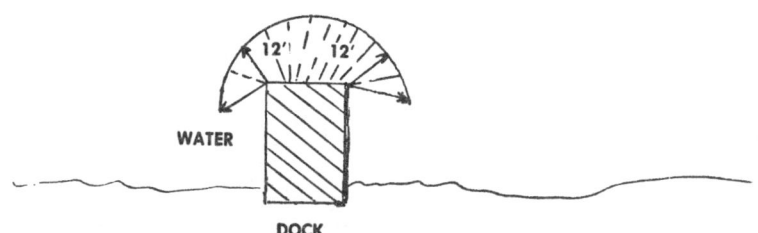

Area to be covered is 12 feet in all directions of dock left all the way around to right.

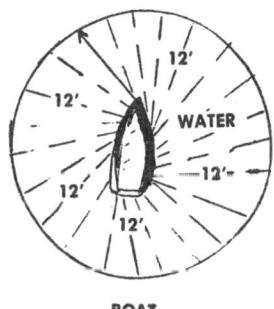

Area to be covered is 12 feet in a complete circle. (This takes in a lot of surface area)

Continue to work out and in through a complete circle. Direct your light on a spot in front of your location. Work crab in and towards you.

FIGURE 1   **NIGHT CRABBING**

CHAPTER 10

SUMMARY

The many varied and different methods and techniques of **HOW TO CATCH A CRAB,** have been depicted in Part II. After studying these methods and with a minimum of practice, the crabber should have sufficient knowledge and be able to master the "how to" part of each. Just as important as the **How to Use a Method** is the **When to Use a Method.** In other words, which method should be selected and used under a multitude of prevailing circumstances and conditions that may be encountered at any time and in any location? Acknowledgment must be given to state laws as well as to the weather, tides, water temperatures and depths because some, any or all of these conditions may restrict each of these crabbing methods at times. The author has consolidated the following specific information as a guide and permanent reference to aid the crabber in making the best choice:

1. **Hand Lines:** Should be used only:
   (a) When the surface water is calm.
   (b) When the surface water is not choppy.
   (c) When there is little or no wind.
   (d) When the water is reasonably clear.
   (e) When the water is shallow (one to twelve feet).
   (f) When the water temperatures are between 62° and 80°F.
   (g) When it is not raining.
   (h) When it is not too foggy
   (i) When tides are not running too fast.
   (j) When the state law permits this method.

2. **Trotlines:** Should be used only:
   (a) When surface water is reasonably calm.
   (b) When the surface water is not choppy.
   (c) When the wind is not too strong.
   (d) When, in shallow water, the temperature of the water is between 62^0 and 80^0F.
   (e) When, in deep water, any time is satisfactory if surface meets the above conditions.
   (f) When water is reasonably clear.
   (g) When it is not raining.
   (h) When the state law permits; otherwise, a license must be obtained.
3. **Traps.** Should be used only:
   (a) When line is long enough for trap to reach the bottom.
   (b) When, in shallow water, the water temperature is between 62^0 and 80^0F.
   (c) When, in deep water — anytime.
   (d) When the state law permits; otherwise, a license must be obtained.
4. **Pots:** Should be used only:
   (a) When marked by a buoy.
   (b) When attended (pulled) regularly (one to three days).
   (c) When the state law permits; otherwise, a license must be obtained.

PART III

HANDLING, COOKING, CLEANING, EATING, STORING, AND RECIPES

CHAPTER 1

HOW TO HANDLE CRABS FROM THE BASKET TO THE COOKING POT

Prior to your departure for home, water down your basket or bag full of crabs well and place the basket or bag in the car (see Part II, Chapter 1). Crabs can live out of water for quite some time but if the journey home is over two hours long and the weather extremely hot, many will not survive their "first and last land tour." If possible, and as an extra precaution, place cracked ice on top of the covered crabs. This action will keep the crabs cool and the melting ice will continuously drip down and keep them wet, thus prolonging their demise until their fate is sealed in the "cooking pot." Upon arriving at your destination with your catch, someone will have to transfer the live crabs from the basket to the cooking pot. This job will probably be **yours** - yes, **yours** — so be prepared to apply yourself.

First, it is advisable to wash and clean the crabs off before plunging them into the boiling water. This procedure can be accomplished by: (1) lightly watering them while in the basket with a garden hose; (2) dumping the basket of crabs into a large metal tub containing water; or (3) depositing the crabs into a deep-well sink (usually the kitchen sink) and allowing cold water to flow gently over the crabs. Not much rinsing is required. After the crabs have been rinsed, you will undoubtedly find some crabs that have not survived the trip home. They, unfortunately, expired "en route." Remove and dispose of the dead crabs. It is strongly suggested that you do not cook the dead ones even though crabs can be cooked and eaten up to four hours after they have expired. Deterioration takes place and bacteria multiplies rapidly in dead shellfish, so why take a chance of becoming ill? A word to the wise is sufficient: **Cook only live crabs.**

When the water is boiling, pick up the crabs, one by one, either by using bare hands (if you are brave and quick), a heavy pair of gloves, or tongs (Part II, Chapter 1) and plunge each crab into the boiling, rolling water head first and upside down (belly up). This act is **not** inhuman. The crab dies immediately without realizing what has taken place. Occasionally when picking up a crab, other crabs will be holding on to it and you will come up with a "string of crabs". Try to shake these clinging crabs off, but if you are not successful, make sure all are alive and then drop the whole string into the boiling water. Don't be too concerned if their claws fall off upon entering the water. This happens when they are not dropped in "belly up." After all of the crabs have been transferred to the pot, your job is over — not too difficult a process after all.

More than likely, during this converting period (transferring crabs to the pot), you will attract an audience of those not as brave or reckless as you who will laugh at and criticize your caution, your quick movements and perhaps your clumsy ineptness in handling these clawing creatures. If this audience proves too much of a disturbance for your nerves, you can end the annoyances quickly by going after the culprits with crab in hand. The laughter will immediately change to shrieks, the criticism will abruptly cease, and there will be a rapid and total exodus from the kitchen. The last laugh is always the best!

CHAPTER 2

COOKING HARD-SHELL CRABS

Hard-shell crabs must always be cooked before the meat can be removed from the body; generally, this is done by boiling the hardshell crabs. Fill your pot with enough water so that when the crabs are plunged in, they will be completely covered. The size of the pot and the size of the crabs determine how many can fit into your particular pot. You may have to use several pots, and several cookings may be necessary if a twenty-gallon pot is not available. As a rule of thumb, one and one-fourth gallons of water should be used for each two-gallon pot capacity. This ratio will cook two to three Dungeness crabs and ten to twelve blue claw crabs. It follows then that a six-gallon pot will take three and three-fourths gallons of water and will cook six to eight Dungeness crabs or thirty to thirty-six blue claw crabs; a ten-gallon pot will take six and one-fourth gallons of water and cook ten to twelve Dungeness and forty to forty-eight blue claw crabs.

Directions:
To each gallon of water (stale beer may be substituted for some of the water), add one-half cup of vinegar or lemon juice (two tablespoons per quart), one-fourth cup of salt (one tablespoon per quart) and one-half to one tablespoon of dried mustard. These are the required basic ingredients. However, depending upon your tastes and culinary aptitude, you may, if you like, also add any or all of the following spices (two to three dashes per gallon): cracked red pepper (six to eight

peppercorns), black pepper, celery seed, mace, sage, ginger, thyme, laurel leaves, paprika, cinnamon and several bay leaves.

After your ingredients have been added and the water has reached a rolling boil, plunge in the crabs one by one as described in Part III, Chapter 1. Cook crabs at a boil for fifteen to twenty minutes (usually eighteen minutes is just fine). The crabs will turn completely red. Remove the crabs from the boiling water after they are cooked and then let stand in cold water until they are cool enough to handle. Then clean or place in the refrigerator until ready to clean, eat or use (see Chapter 3 following). Boiled crabs are normally eaten cold when eaten directly from the shell.

Steamed Hard-shell Crabs:

There is almost nothing quite as delicious as feasting on hot steamed Maryland-style crabs, picked and eaten right out of the shells—good but hot!

Directions:

For each dozen of blue claw hard-shell crabs, use one cup of water and one cup of vinegar, which should be put in container first. Then place crabs on elevated platform in container and generously sprinkle seasoning over each layer of crabs. Steam about twenty minutes and eat when hot. The dried seasoning may be purchased at your local fish market or you may make your own mixture. Five ounces of dried mixture is sprinkled on each dozen of blue claw crabs.

Steamed Crab Mixture:

Makes two pounds of mix (good for six dozen crabs).

1 lb. coarse salt (small rock salt)
5 oz. crushed red pepper
3 oz. dried mustard
1½ oz. ginger
1 oz. black pepper
1 oz. celery flakes
1 oz. onion flakes
½ oz. celery seeds
½ oz. crushed bay leaves
½ oz. laurel leaves
½ oz. cinnamon
½ oz. paprika
½ oz. thyme
½ oz. mace

Mix all ingredients well and store in airtight jar until ready to use.

The foregoing cooking procedures apply to all edible hard-shell crabs (Dungeness, red, rock, or blue claw).

CHAPTER 3

CLEANING, PICKING, REMOVING THE MEAT AND EATING HARD - AND SOFT - SHELL CRABS

After the hard-shell crabs have been cooked (boiled) and are cool enough to handle, the crab meat must be removed from the shell. Although the cleaning and picking process is quite time consuming and also a little messy, it is not at all difficult when you know how to do it. Before you start, it is important to prepare the working area, and to have the necessary tools and utensils available and at your disposal. Clear the working area, such as a table, and cover it with heavy brown paper or newspapers; then place a large bowl on the table (this is to hold the crab meat). You will also need a paring knife, a spoon, a fork and a nut pick to aid in removing the crab meat, a wooden cutting board for hammering and cracking the claws, a small wooden mallet, pliers, a small piece of a broom handle or nut cracker (for cracking the shells), and a large plastic refuse or garbage bag to hold the discarded shells and waste materials. Now you are all set for the "cleaning and picking."

Instructions: (see Figure 1)

Step 1: Take a crab, lay it on its back, belly up, and with the point of the knife or fingers, lift up the apron (Flap A), break it off and discard.

Step 2: Turn the crab over, claws away from you, flat fins nearest to you. With thumb or point of knife, lift up and pull off the top shell and discard.

Step 3: Next, with your fingers or knife, scrape off the six gills (lungs, sometimes called the dead meat) on either side of the open body (C and D). These gills are not edible, so dicard.

Step 4: With thumb and forefinger, press down and break off mouth area (E) and discard.

Step 5: The yellow, green, red, orange or brownish-colored material found just behind the mouth area (F) is the fat, heart and/or the eggs (roe) of the crab and is good to eat. In fact, gourmets find it delicious. Spoon this material out and place in separate bowl if you wish to eat it as is, or mix it with the crab meat when stuffing a lobster or fish. If you decide not to use it, wash it out over the sink.

Step 6: Break off all legs and claws next to body, and put aside for cracking and removal of meat later.

Step 7: Hold crab body at each side and break apart at center, then break each half in half again. The meat under the membrane covering will be exposed and can be removed by the fingers, a fork, or a nut pick. Make sure to remove all transparent membranes (cartilage) before placing meat in the bowl or eating.

Crack all claws with mallet, pliers or nut crackers and remove meat. Dungeness crab legs contain a lot of meat and these should be cracked and the meat removed. The blue claw crab legs contain very little meat; but if you wish, you can break a leg at the top joint and squeeze or suck a little meat out.

About eighteen or twenty blue claw crabs when cleaned will produce a pound of crab meat (two cups). One Dungeness crab weighing two to three pounds before cleaning will supply almost a pound of solid crab meat when cleaned.

When all the crabs have been cleaned and picked, you can either prepare the dish of your choice (see Chapter 5) or else freeze the meat, or excess meat, as described in Chapter 4.

Soft-Shell Crabs:

Live soft-shell crabs are either broiled, fried or deep-fried, but must be prepared as follows before using: Remember you are handling a live, soft-shell crab—but don't be afraid, as soft crabs cannot bite. Kill soft-shell crabs by sticking a point of a knife or an ice pick between the eyes.

Instructions: (see Figure 2)

Step 1: Lay soft-shell crab on its back (belly up) and remove apron (A).

Step 2: Turn crab over, lift up the pointed ends (spikes) and remove the six gills on each side. Then replace each point to its original position.

Step 3: With scissors, cut off mouth, eyes and feelers (C). Wash thoroughly. Now your soft-shell crab is ready. Dip in egg and cracker meal and fry, deep-fry or broil. You are in for a real treat!

Live Hard Crabs:

Kill crabs by sticking pointed knife or ice pick between the eyes. Remove claws and legs and clean body as described in Step 1 through Step 5. Cook or freeze (see Chapters 4 and 5).

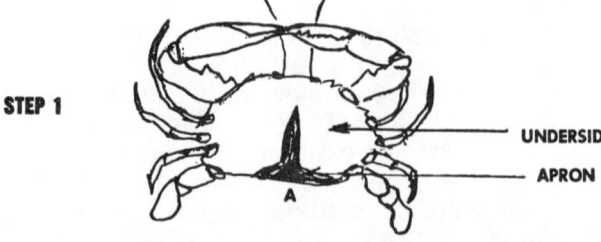

UNDERSIDE

APRON

With crab on back (belly-up) lift up apron flap A, with fingers or knife point, break off and discard.

STEP 2

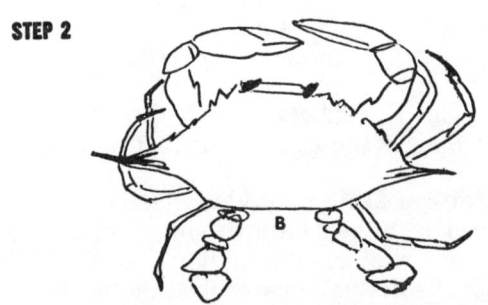

Turn crab over, claws away from you, flat fins nearest you.

With thumb or knife point, lift up and remove top shell and discard.

FIGURE 1   **HARD SHELL CRAB**

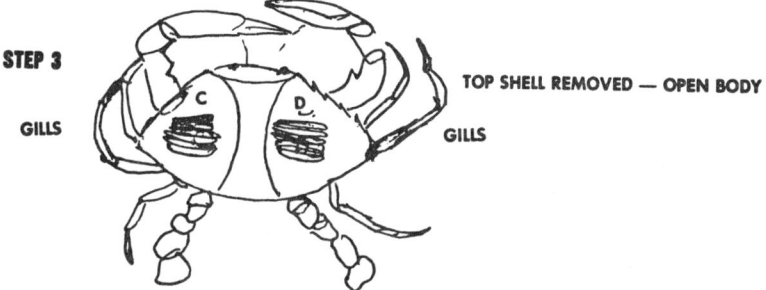

STEP 3

GILLS

C

D

TOP SHELL REMOVED — OPEN BODY

GILLS

With fingers or knife scrape off 6 gills on each side C and D,
remove and discard.

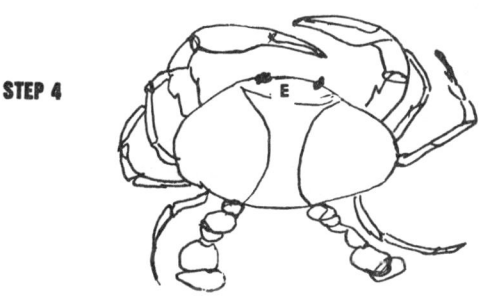

STEP 4

E

With thumb and forefinger press down and break off mouth
area E and discard.

FIGURE 1   **HARD SHELL CRAB**

STEP 5

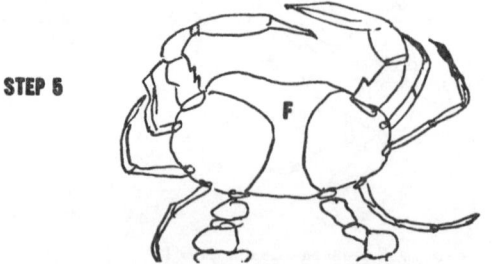

The material in Area F is good to eat, spoon out and save or wash out under faucet.

STEP 6

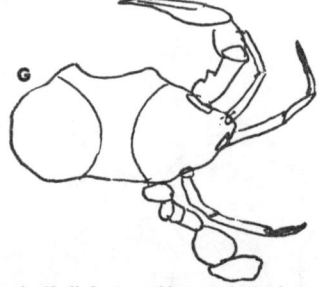

Break off all claws and legs at the body G, and put aside for cracking and removal of meat later.

STEP 7

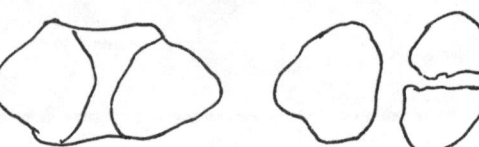

Hold body with both hands and break apart at center, then break each half again and remove all meat from the transparent membranes.

FIGURE 1

STEP 1

UNDERSIDE

APRON

With soft shell crab on back (belly-up) remove apron A and discard.

STEP 2

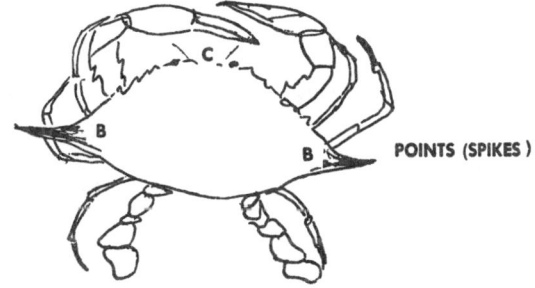

POINTS (SPIKES)

Lift up points of shell at B, remove gills on either side under paper shell. Place shell back in position.

With scissor cut off eyes, mouth and feelers C. Crab is ready.

FIGURE 2   **SOFT SHELL CRAB**

117

CHAPTER 4

HOW TO STORE AND FREEZE CRABS

Cooked shellfish is very perishable and since the meat spoils quickly it should be used immediately or as soon as possible after it is cooked. Whole crabs or solid meat will only last two days or three days at most under refrigeration; however, if properly wrapped and frozen, it will keep up to three months in the freezer.

Hard-shell crabs can be frozen when (1) alive and whole; (2) cooked and whole; (3) cleaned as in Step 1 through Step 6 (bodies and claws), Figure 1, Chapter 3; or (4) as solid crab meat in portions. Soft-shell crabs can be frozen alive, as is, or prepared following directions in Step 1 through Step 3 (see Figure 2, Chapter 3).

When whole crab or crab meat is frozen quickly, there is less danger of contamination from spoilage organisms or from the action of enzymes that cause deterioration in appearance and flavor. Do not let crabs stand at room temperature too long before freezing.

There are many types of wrappings and containers. Food dries out in a freezer unless carefully wrapped; it also expands, so allow some room for expansion. When freezing crabs or crab meat, use freezer bags, moisture-vapor-proof cellophane, aluminum foil or pail pack. Label every package. Indicate the contents, date, weight, or other important information. Special stamps, labels, pencils, pens, and tape for this purpose are available. Use packages with the oldest dates first.

Freeze crabs or crab meat promptly after wrapping or packaging. Put in freezer at once. If taken to a locker plant, it should be carried in an insulated bag or box or wrapped in several layers of heavy paper. Do not permit package to stand at room temperature.

Temperature of freezing is important. Crabs and crab meat should be frozen and stored at 0^0 to -5^0 F.

When the frozen crabs or crab meat is removed from the freezer, you can cook meat thawed or partially thawed. Cook thawed crabs and meat at once. Allow more time for cooking at a lower temperature when starting your crab dish from a partially frozen state.

Never refreeze crabs or crab meat unless there is still some ice visible on the package.

CHAPTER 5
SOME FAVORITE RECIPES

Crab meat is one of the finest-tasting shellfish found on this earth — a luxury on any table, a delight to any gourmet. Crab meat can be prepared in innumerable ways. The succulent and delicious palate-pleasing flavor comes through in each dish to win the praises of everyone who is fortunate enough to share this epicurean treat. Crab meat can be eaten hot or cold, out of the shell, plain, with sauces or melted butter, steamed, broiled, baked, fried or prepared as described in the following recipes.

Cooks, attention! Try an adventure in culinary artistry.

DEVILED CRAB

3 tablespoons butter
2 tablespoons onion, finely chopped
1 teaspoon Worcester—shire sauce
3 tablespoons flour
1 teaspoon dry mustard
Red or black pepper, few grains
½ teaspoon paprika
¾ teaspoon salt
2 to 3 cups cooked crab meat
1 cup milk
½ cup cream
½ cup grated cheese
½ cup buttered crumbs

Heat butter; add onion and cook over low heat until onion is soft but not browned. Blend in flour and seasoning. Slowly add milk and cook, stirring constantly over low heat until thickened. Add cream. Remove from heat.

Pick over crab meat to remove any cartilage membrane that may have been missed in cleaning. Add to hot sauce.

Fill crab shells (washed and scrubbed) or cooking shells. Sprinkle with buttered crumbs, grated cheese and a dash of paprika.

Bake in moderate oven (375⁰F.) for twenty to twenty-five minutes until brown. This makes six servings. Add five or six shakes of hot sauce to crab meat if you like your deviled crab hotter.

CRAB MEAT AU GRATIN

Pick over two cups of crab meat and remove cartilage.

Combine with two cups of medium white sauce, one and one-half tablespoons lemon juice, one and one-half teaspoons grated onion. Turn into greased casserole; top with buttered crumbs and paprika (add a little grated cheese if desired). Bake in moderate oven (375°F.) for twenty or twenty-five minutes or until browned. This makes six to eight servings.

CRAB MEAT NEWBURG

1 cup cream or evaporated milk
1 teaspoon Worchestershire sauce
1 tablespoon (or more) sherry wine
3 tablespoons butter or margarine

¾ teaspoon salt
½ teaspoon paprika
⅛ teaspoon nutmeg
2 egg yolks
6 slices buttered toast
2 cups cooked crab meat

Heat the cream with the butter in top part of a double boiler. Add crab, salt, paprika and nutmeg. Beat egg yolks; add Worcestershire sauce and sherry wine and mix a little hot liquid with the yolks. Pour the egg mixture into the sauce. Cook one or two minutes more over simmering water. Serve on toast. This makes four to six servings.

CRAB MEAT SOUP

1 can condensed green pea soup
1 cup crab meat (cooked)
1 cup milk

1 can condensed tomato soup
¼ cup evaporated milk
¼ cup sherry wine

Combine pea soup, milk and tomato soup in saucepan and blend thoroughly. Flake crab meat and add. Cook and stir over low heat. Add sherry when hot. Do not boil. Serves four persons.

CRAB CASSEROLE

1 pound (2—3 cups) cooked crab meat
1 small can mushrooms (don't drain)
1 can drained peas

1 can celery, chicken or mushroom soup
1 small can pimentos (cut up)
1 can whole kernel corn
Pepper to taste

Mix all ingredients, place in Pyrex dish and cover with bread crumbs that have been slightly buttered. Bake at 350°F. for forty minutes. This serves six persons.

CRAB CAKES NEW ORLEANS

1½ tablespoons lemon juice
2 cups cooked crab meat
¼ teaspoon pepper

1 teaspoon salt
4 eggs (separated)
½ teaspoon dry mustard
1/3 cup chopped onion
2 tablespoons butter

Pick over crab meat; remove any cartilage. Beat egg yolks until thick and lemon-colored. Fold in crab meat. Heat butter, add onions and cook over low heat about ten minutes, or until soft and lightly browned. Stir into crab meat. Add lemon juice, mustard, salt and pepper. Beat white of eggs until stiff but not dry. Fold into the crab mixture. Drop by spoonfuls into hot buttered skillet and brown lightly on both sides. Serve with tartar sauce. Makes six to eight servings.

CRAB MEAT SOUFFLE'

1 tablespoon parsley, finely chopped	¼ teaspoon cream of tartar
	1 cup cooked crab meat
1 cup thick white sauce	4 eggs, separated
1 tablespoon lemon juice	1½ teaspoons grated onion
½ teaspoon paprika	

Pick over crab meat to remove cartilage, and flake. Add crab meat to white sauce, followed by lemon juice, egg yolks (beaten until thick and lemon-colored), onion, parsley, and paprika. Allow to cool. Beat egg whites until frothy; add cream of tartar and continue beating until stiff but not dry. Fold into crab meat mixture.

Turn into greased (buttered) casserole, one and one-half quart capacity. Bake in moderate oven (325°F.) about one hour. Makes four to six servings.

CRAB CHOW MEIN

2 tablespoons melted butter or margarine	1 pound can bean sprouts (drained)
2 cans chinese noodles (5—oz. cans)	1 can mushroom soup
	1 green pepper, chopped
8 stalks celery, chopped	2 cups crab meat (cooked)
2 medium onions, chopped	

Cook celery, green peppers, and onion in melted fat until tender. Add bean sprouts and crab meat. Heat. Pour mushroom soup over top and simmer for ten minutes. Serve on crisp noodles. Serves six.

CRABS ITALIAN

18—24 fresh crab bodies (uncooked)	¼ cup olive oil
	1 tablespoon oregano
6 cloves of garlic, cut and diced	

Place uncooked crab bodies in Pyrex dish or shallow pan. Sprinkle with olive oil, add diced garlic. Sprinkle with oregano. Bake in oven (400°F.) until done, approximately forty-five minutes. This is very good. Crab bodies may also be broiled in a period of only fifteen or twenty minutes, basting occasionally.

CRABS IN BLANKETS

½ pound cooked crab meat (1 to 2 cups)
1 tablespoon minced parsley
1/3 cup celery, chopped fine
1 tablespoon lemon juice
Salt and pepper to taste
1/3 cup toasted chopped almonds
1 doz. thin slices of ham
1 8-oz. package cream cheese

Blend crab and all ingredients (except ham) in softened cream cheese. Then spread the mixture on each ham slice and secure with tooth pick. Chill several hours. Remove picks before serving. Serve with a luncheon before the salad or with a buffet spread.

CRAB LOUIS (SALAD)

1 pound cooked crab meat
4 medium tomatoes, peeled
4 cups torn lettuce leaves
2 hard-boiled eggs

Flake crab meat, leaving large pieces of leg or claw meat unbroken for garnish. Mound the crab meat on the lettuce (arrange on salad plates). Quarter the hard-boiled eggs, and cut the tomatoes into wedges. Arrange in a circle around the mound of crab meat. Serve with Louis dressing (see below). Serves four.

LOUIS DRESSING

2 tablespoons chili sauce or tomato catsup
2 tablespoons heavy cream
2 tablespoons minced onions
½ teaspoon Worchestershire sauce
½ cup mayonnaise
1 tablespoon lemon juice
Salt and pepper

Mix all ingredients except salt and pepper. Season to taste. For an extra taste treat, add one-half avocado, mashed, to the mixture. Makes one cup.

SOFT-SHELL CRABS

Clean as described in Chapter 3, dip in egg and cracker meal. Fry, deep-fry or broil for ten minutes (five minutes on each side) and season to taste.

BOILED OR STEAMED CRABS

See Part III, Chapter 2, for cooking instructions and mixes.

GLOSSARY

1. Abdomen — The tail of the crab
2. Appendages — Legs, attached to the body
3. Arthropod — Joint-limbed animal
4. Autogeny — Act of regeneration, growing back new claws and legs
5. Ballie — Sponge crab, a female with an egg mass beneath the abdomen
6. Berried crab or crab in berry — Sponge crab
7. Blue or blue claw crab — Callinectes sapidus(type found on the East Coast)
8. Brackish — Applied to water mixed with salt . . . seawater, not too salty
9. Buck and rider — Pair of mating crabs; A "Doubler"
10. Buckram crab — One having a pliable, leathery shell, following the soft-shell condition
11. Buffalo crab — Soft crab with large claw missing (often lost in shedding)
12. Busted sook — Sponge Crab
13. Buster — Shedding crab which is beginning to emerge from its shell
14. Cannibalistic — To eat each other
15. Carapace — The shell of a crustacean
16. Channeler or chandler — A large male crab that remains in the deeper water (channels) of a river during the summer; a Jimmy crab
17. Coconut crab — A land crab, living in tropical regions; member of Gecarcinidae family
18. Crab ring — Form of trap used to catch crabs
19. Crustacea — A large class of arthropods, almost all aquatic
20. Cushion crab — Sponge crab
21. Doubler — Pair of mating crabs; buck and rider
22. Dungeness crab — Cancer magister, found on the West Coast
23. Ecodysis — Act of moulting
24. Egg—bearing — Female crab with sponge
25. Estuary — The wide lower part of a river where it becomes tidal

26. External skeleton or exo-skeleton	Outer shell of the crab
27. Fat crab, green crab, or snot crab	These terms are used by most watermen when referring to a crab approaching the shedding period and showing a "white-rim" color sign. Also used in referring to any hard crab with firm meat.
28. Green crab	White-rim crab
29. Hand line	Line used to catch crabs, usually tied with weight and bait
30. Hand dip trotline	Long line with baits attached; used to catch crabs with a scoop or dip net
31. Hard or hard—shell crab	Crabs with a hard shell following the Buckram condition
32. Hermit crab	Not a true crab; a member of the Anomura classification
33. Horseshoe crab	Non-edible, being used in many laboratory experiments today
34. Jimmy crab, Jimmy dick or Jimmy channeler	A very large male blue claw crab, sometimes used in crab pots with claws removed to attract female crabs for mating
35. Keepers	Legal size crabs that may be kept — the ones that are taken
36. King crab	Paralithodes camtshatica, or Japanese crab; not a true crab but caught commercially for the claws
37. Land crab	Those crabs that live on land, coconut and robber crabs
38. Lemon crab	Sponge crab
39. Megalops	Crab larva, between the Zoeal and crab stage
40. Moult, molt	To shed; to back out of old shell
41. Nicking a crab	To break the removable fingers of the claws to prevent the use of the claws as pincers
42. Orange crab	Sponge crab
43. Paper—shell or paper—back crab	Having a fairly hard shell which is easily cracked following the buckram stage
44. Paramoeba or amoebiasis	Gray crab disease
45. Patent trotlines	Those trotlines used with patented net or catcher operated from a boom on a boat

46. Peeler crab	Hard crab having a fully formed soft-shell beneath the hard outer shell; a red-sign crab, sometimes applied to the white-rim, pink-rim and red-sign crabs.
47. Phylum	Any primary division of the animal kingdom
48. Pink—rim	Following the white-rim condition, crab expected to shed within a week
49. Plankton	Minute or microscopic aquatic, living animals
50. Pods	A mass of immature king crabs, formed for self-protection
51. Pots	A form of trap to catch crabs
52. Punk	Sponge crab
53. Red crab	Edible crab found on both coasts, usually in deep water. Known as Cancer productus
54. Red—sign peeler	Following pink-rim stage
55. Regenerate	To grow back a claw or an appendage
56. Robber crab	Land crab, not a true crab
57. Rock crab	Sometimes referred to as a red crab (Cancer irroatus)
58. Sally crab	Young female, an immature female
59. Scoop or dip net	A long- or shorthandled net used to scoop or dip crabs out of the water
60. Seine	A large net used to catch fish or crabs
61. Shed	The casting-off of a shell; moulting
62. Snoods	Small lines tied to a trotline on which the bait is tied
63. Snot crabs	White-rim crab named because of the watery substance which issues from the break of the crab claws when they are nicked
64. Soft crab, soft shell crab, or softie	A crab that has just emerged from the old, hard shell and has a new, soft, pliable shell
65. Sook	An adult female crab
66. Spikes	Points of the blue claw crab
67. Sponge crab, ballie, berried crab	Names given to the female crab carrying an egg mass on the abdomen

68. Stone crab	Menippe mercenaria found along the southern coast and sought primarily for their claws
69. Swimming paddles	The rear flat legs of the crab; last pair of legs
70. Throw backs	Crabs that are undersize, illegal by state laws, or that you do not keep
71. Traps	Crabbing gear or equipment used to trap and catch crabs
72. Trash fish	Those fish normally not eaten by humans such as sea robins and oyster crackers
73. Whale	Name given to large soft-shell crab
74. White—rim crab	The fat, green or snot crab condition. There is a thin white line along the inner border of the back (flat) fin. Crab expected to shed within two weeks
75. Whitey	Name sometimes given to a crab that has shed some three days to two weeks before; the underneath is white, and body contains very little meat
76. Zoea	The larvae that hatches from the crab egg

SELECTED BIBLIOGRAPHY

"A Commentary on Claw Deformities in the Blue Crab." **Esturine Bulletin,** June 1963. Vol. VII, No. 2 and 3, pages 15-23.

"A New Species of Paramoeba **(Amoebia Paramoebiae)** Parasitic in the Crab, Callinectes sapidus." Reprinted from **Journal of Invertebrate Pathology,** September 1969. Vol. XIV, No. 2.

Brown, F.A. Jr. **Selected Invertebrate Types.** 1967.

Bushman, Ralph. **Animals without Backbones.** Revised edition. 1938.

Fluctuations in Abundance of the Blue Crab in the Chesapeake Bay. Research Report 14. Fish and Wildlife Service, U.S. Department of the Interior.

Lutz, Frank: Welch, Paul S.; Galtsoff, Paul S.; Needham, James G., Chairman. **Culture Methods for Invertebrate Animals 1937.** (Made possible by a grant from the Research Council.)

Meglitch, Paul A. **Invertebrate Zoology.** 2nd Edition. 1972.

"Old Blue Claws." **New Jersey Outdoors.** Reprinted from the July 1955 issue.

Van Engel, W.A. "The Blue Crab and Its Fishery in the Chesapeake Bay, Part I, Reproduction, Early Development, Growth and Migration." **Commercial Fisheries Review.** Vol. XX, No. 6. Fish and Wildlife Service, U.S. Department of the Interior.

"Types of Gear for Hard Crab Fishing." **Commercial Fisheries** Review. Vol. XXIV, No. 9 Fish and Wildlife Service, U.S. Department of the Interior.